Intra-Educational Classism: How the Liberal Middle Classes Dominate the Working Classes in Education

By

Benton Fazzolari, PhD

Table of Contents

Chapter 1: Diversity, Inclusion, & Cultural Responsivity: Zaretta Hammond's Problematic Text

Innumerable pedagogical texts address diversity. Educators and educational institutions show a high level of concern about all aspects of diversity. Ideally, educators should display sensitivity, respect, recognition, understanding, and empathy for diversity because "diversity" connotes a position of marginalization, oppression, and victimization. In fact, many, if not all, job applications for educators ask prospective employees about their commitment to diversity. Some educators may struggle to find an appropriate answer to these questions and may find it difficult to articulate tangible pedagogical strategies, activities, and personal participation that emphasize their support for diversity in education. Others may find these questions easy to answer. Many educators simply appear to support diversity, by default, because they represent one or more of the standard models of diversity such as race, ethnicity, and gender identity. Many educators appear against diversity by default because they do not represent any of the models of diversity (e.g. heterosexual white men).

Furthermore, diversity appears as a tiered system through which identity models are compared and ranked. The more models of diversity represented by a person's identity, the higher ranked the person sits on the tiered system of diversity. Obviously, White men rank the lowest while a combination of models may rank the highest. This appears to be the standard mechanism used to determine notions of diversity. These notions sometimes determine things like speech, hiring, promotions, and other basic functions that relate to navigation within educational bureaucracies. It is important to note that class status is one central category of identification that is not included in categories of diversity.

Issues arise within this structure. For example, some may not represent a model of diversity by default but may be far more active in their support of diversity than some who, by default, represent one or more of the models of diversity. Perhaps those who, by default, do not represent one or more of the models of diversity must prove their commitment to diversity while those who, by default, represent one or more of the models of diversity simply appear as committed to diversity and, therefore, do not have the compulsion to prove anything.

To further complicate things, class status lacks definitive representation in the modeling structure of diversity. Therefore, educators do not comprehensively grasp models of diversity and their convergence with the existing concrete economic conditions informed by capitalism. In other words, perhaps educators should maneuver away from ideological notions of diversity into material notions of diversity and its interplay with capitalism.

Of course, this is not simple. To understand diversity within capitalism complicates the issue. For instance, how do we understand diversity if a Hispanic woman or nonwhite transgender person is fully committed to the dictates of capitalism? How do we identify someone as diverse if that person supports an economic structure that has traditionally marginalized and oppressed diverse peoples? What do we make of diversity if people of color or LGBTQ people support the MAGA movement? Furthermore, as capitalism develops, it expands to include all the models of diversity, e.g. inclusion. Diversity in advertising makes this obvious. In addition, some of the most cutthroat capitalists in the world have received awards for their dedication to diversity models. Goldman Sachs serves as one example. They ranked second in Financial Services for LGBT+ inclusion, ninth in Best Finance Companies for women, a one hundred percent rating on the Disability Equality Index as well as being honored as Best of the Best for employers of Asian-Americans.[1] As capitalism advances, notions of diversity become more complicated, particularly if diversity models contain any conceptions of liberation or transformation against capitalism. In addition, at what point do the models of diversity no longer connote marginalization, oppression, and victimization if / when they become fully embraced, embedded, and included by capitalists?

Consequently, two factors undermine diversity in capitalism. One includes the co-optation of diverse people(s) and the other includes defining diversity, itself, within the boundaries of capitalism. Jean Baudrillard highlights this in his book *The Consumer Society* when he writes, "The real differences which characterized persons made them contradictory beings."[2] The massive and ongoing global campaign (colonialism, imperialism, neocolonialism, globalization, etc.), eliminates diversity in any meaningful sense. Capitalism materially and objectively summons diverse peoples into the capitalist economy while, paradoxically, diverse peoples fight for inclusion into the same capitalist economy. This holds true on all levels of the economic pyramid whether in high paying employment in business and technology or in low paying employment like farm work or policing. Cornel West refers to this as "buying them off."[3]

When capitalists purchase the labor power of diverse peoples (or when diverse peoples win their right to sell their labor power to capitalists) inclusion appears, e.g. Goldman Sachs. This allows for cutthroat capitalists to present a glossy image of their practices while they crush the contradictory aspects of authentic diversity. Obviously, the highly publicized fight for inclusion into all aspects of the capitalist system further problematizes models of diversity as vectors of liberation or anti-establishment transformation and challenges the claims of marginalization, oppression, and victimization. The microscopic spectrum of diversity, as simply a series of surface models, appears to exist harmoniously with capitalism. This presents a real problem against actual economic change as current liberal perspectives fight for inclusion of diversity models into the very system that not only produces these diversity models but also systematically, objectively, and materially eliminates authentic global and domestic diversity (e.g. Amazonian peoples forced out of the rainforest and into the urban workforce). This contradiction appears most apparent in the proximity of liberal managerial and administrative professionals (perhaps most obviously in educational contexts). Diversity models simply become an addition to the existing ruling hierarchy and economic order.

To be clear, perhaps the appropriate aim should be to generate real diversity and/or create the material conditions where real diversity can (re)emerge. Simply put, we must focus on the overcoming of capitalism rather than the inclusion into capitalism. For instance, what if all of the aims of social justice were met tomorrow, but the material conditions of capitalism remained? To be more specific, a nonwhite transgender person may go to an office to work with the freedom and safety to be transgendered but must still go to the office to sell labor-power to capitalists and will still live within the dictates of precarious employment that proliferates in capitalism. On a broader level, the inclusion into capitalism still leaves a mass of hyper-exploited workers all over the world. Hence, anti-capitalism should foreground liberation and transformation.

In education, this presents a tricky predicament because of the hierarchal and technocratic structure of educational institutions. In the most basic terms, those with secure positions (tenured faculty, department chairs, deans, etc.) appear unlikely to risk their security for anti-capitalist activity, particularly when it conflicts with their own economic interests. This is obvious in labor relations, e.g. adjunct vs. tenured or department chairs vs. deans and so on. The material hierarchal (social) relationships determine the political engagement of people in education. They overwhelm concepts of integrity, ethics, morality, justice, etc. It is very easy for administrative professionals (presidents, deans, department chairs, etc.) to fight for inclusion of diversity models into educational institutions, but it is very hard for administrative professionals to fight for guaranteed employment for adjuncts and other insecure laborers, and, more significantly, it directly conflicts with the technocratic role, requirements, objectives, and mandates of the administrative professionals. Hence, social justice can exist at every level of the hierarchy in liberal departments and institutions, but not anti-capitalism or economic justice. As illustrated above, this is because what appears as a struggle for social justice in the form of diversity and inclusion is actually just the expansion of the capitalist mode of production and its social relations.

In reality, the struggle requires a more radical strategy to transform education with the aim toward eliminating economic classes. Without entirely realizing it, liberal educators and administrators subtly aim to increase the power of capital and reinforce its power over alternative ways of being in the world (actual conflictual diversity). They do this by advertising an artificial or superficial form of diversity easily digested by themselves and the capitalist establishment. Baudrillard's description of the Tasaday peoples who were discovered in the Philippines serves as an apt comparison to the liberal inclusion practices by contemporary educators. He notes that upon the insistence of the anthropologists who discovered them, the Tasaday were returned to the jungle because the anthropologists "were seeing the indigenous people disintegrate immediately upon contact."[4] Essentially, the disintegration period has already passed in global diversity and has birthed diversity models. The alternative ways of being in the world have already been destroyed and every people has been discovered. The trace of difference present in contemporary American culture represents mostly consumerist differences, and/or sanitized versions of formerly deeply rooted and authentic cultural ways of being. In essence, diversity simply means including peoples whose differences have already been eliminated in order to posture an appearance of difference in an ocean of sameness. Just like the Tasaday, we have disintegrated, but are continually reintegrated into capitalist circuits and, thereby, lose any connection to any pre-capitalist (or potential post-capitalist) ways of being in the world. The Tasaday offers a much needed perspective of our predicament.

Baudrillard also mentions the discovery and decay of Ramses' mummy. This illustration is even more apt because what constitutes present day concepts of diversity or diversity models are merely mummified or preserved versions of previously contradictory forms of diverse ways of being in the world. The preservation of diversity through commercialized forms offer everyone "capitalist friendly" caricatures of peoples, customs, and practices. If left alone to simply practice their ways of being, global diversity would have remained as preserved as Ramses' mummy, but since global imperialism discovered peoples and set their disintegration in motion, the liberal strategy aims to safely preserve diversity within capitalism and at no risk to their class status. Of course, it goes without saying that conservatives would not and do not even attempt to preserve diversity and are objectively dangerous to local and global diversity.

This does not imply that really existing prejudice against people(s) who carry models of diversity is not a problem in education or in the world outside of education. Ethnic, racial, and gender prejudice certainly exist and must always be resisted. Nonetheless, Baudrillard's examples put liberal notions of diversity into perspective. Hence, we must be honest about the breadth of diversity in a social and cultural field overwhelmed by capitalism rather than safely hide behind popular notions of inclusion. Simply put, middle-class full-time faculty and administrators can easily support diversity and inclusion because their support creates an appearance of concern about equality while it excludes the overt classism and economic injustice embedded in their positions within material educational structures.

Cultural Responsivity

Cultural Responsivity is a popular phrase and concept that floats around various educational settings. It appears on job applications, in professional development programs, educational literature, and academic conference presentations. It is also featured in the 2015 book by Zaretta Hammond entitled, *Culturally Responsive Teaching & the Brain*. It is an extremely popular book in educational circles. The book connects many of the trends that have emerged in other disciplines and practices to education. For example, it includes all of the idealism found in habits of mind, growth and deficit mindsets, neuroplasticity, micro-aggression, mindfulness, and implicit bias. It meanders through notions of cultural practice (deep, shallow, and surface) to bits of neuroscience research (regions of the brain) to practical classroom strategies.

The book's main problem involves its implicit (and sometimes explicit) reinforcement of the capitalist mode of production, material conditions, and subsequent ideology. For example, much of the role of the culturally responsive teacher connects to the commitment to bureaucratic busy work. To explain, Hammond privileges the teacher who is a "warm demander." The warm demander must "acquire the tools to be more data driven in . . . decision-making about learning tactics and strategies . . . through frequent feedback cycles."[5] This locks educators into the role of technicians who facilitate the constant movement of back and forth data. This data functions to normalize, categorize, and hierarchize students who, subsequently, become locked into the counterpart role of young bureaucrats. Obviously, this reminds us of Foucault's assessment of bureaucracy in *Discipline and Punish*. Essentially, the culturally responsive warm demander "supervises every instant . . . [and] compares, differentiates, hierarchizes, homogenizes, [and] excludes" students.[6] Hammond mentions keeping checklists that track student progress toward "learning targets" and to include a space for "students to store their data." This rests in the "individual" goal driven discourse of capital and reproduces the material productive imperatives of the world outside the classroom.

The interest educators and educational institutions have shown in cultural responsivity illustrates its immersion into the capitalist mode of production and its ideology. The hope that teachers will be more efficient and students will be more productive through bureaucratic means fits squarely in how capitalist institutions overwhelm public spaces like schools. Essentially, mass data collection and feedback loops reinforce the power of the capitalist mode of production and reify these capitalist modes of behavior. Teachers and students internalize the values of capitalist managers and administrators. Mark Fisher offers the example of educators who are required to self-assess their performances at work. He writes, "The result is a kind of postmodern capitalist version of Maoist confessionalism, in which workers are required to engage in constant symbolic self-denigration."[7] Therefore, the material conditions of production foreground the ideologically driven practices, which firmly plant educators and students into the capitalist mode of production. Furthermore, since in many or most cases teaching is a precarious job, teachers must abide by these inertial dictates. But more significantly, the activity of data collection and feedback loops reifies the process and the medium.

Additionally, in practical terms, bureaucracy means more work for educators. It takes labor time / power to compose comprehensive reports for individual students and it adds to the tedious tasks students must complete. With the emphasis on data and feedback, the cultural aspect of cultural responsivity appears secondary to the method to produce or the mode of production. The broader and more powerful capitalist culture overwhelms the narrower cultural aspects of race, ethnicity, and gender. In other words, the capitalist mode of production already foregrounds the dominant cultural mode in the culturally responsive educational setting for the individual and the collective. Can an educator maintain an excellent rapport with students while constantly requiring a stream of mutual feedback? Can an educator who perfectly manifests all the positive qualities of a loving, caring, and equitable professional maintain these qualities while engaging in this extremely officious behavior?

Educators might reflect on their own positions in bureaucracies (part of the material structure) to find the answer to these questions. For instance, imagine being on the receiving end of an administrator who requires this time consuming commitment to data and feedback. With materially based hierarchy deeply embedded in the social (professional) relationship, the demand for data and feedback discourages and demoralizes educators. Again, the materially based precariousness of the profession plays a role. In the educator / student relationship, especially with populations of insecure students, will students feel their lack of power and agency inside this material hierarchy, just as precarious educators feel their lack of power and agency in their position to administrators, technicians, and institutions?

Hammond offers the idea of giving wise feedback that involves holding high standards, offering words of encouragement, and giving actionable steps to complete.[8] She further claims that a "warm demander . . . [must] get students to recognize that putting forth the effort is worth the work"[9] and cites a text called *Mindset: The New Psychology of Success*. Her mention of "work" makes one wonder what sort of work is worth working for in a capitalist job market and what sort of working world will students eventually enter to perform this work. The work students complete in school only exhibits its worth in the labor market as long it conforms to and reproduces the dictates of capital and/or the circulation of commodities. This applies to the act of consumption, as well. Hammond implies that success fits within this "work and consume" framework. She also refers to a text which proposes that each individual student will be successful if educators promote a positive mindset. This offers a glimpse into the capitalist mindset of growth of the liberal middle class and enhances the role of capitalist ideology along with materially based bureaucracy.

Later, Hammond offers a chart called "Academic Mindset Components," which exclusively individualizes student brains with phrases like "I can succeed at this," and "My ability and competence grow with my effort." While these may seem benign, these phrases exist through the material conditions of production and mass promotion of hyper-individualism in a capitalist society. Conversely, she specifically mentions the deeply seeded collective and communal worldviews of "Latin American, Asian, African, Middle Eastern, and many Slavic cultures."[10] If we are to be culturally responsive, and the above cultures are deeply collective, then why does she promote and encourage the hyper-individualized pedagogy of "growth mindset"? In addition, and more significantly, this notion of success involves capitalist conceptions like moving up in hierarchal workplaces and socially advancing with more purchasing power in the marketplace. This version of success comes from one specific worldview, thereby negating actual cultural differences through the process of education, itself!

Also important to consider is the implicit and not so implicit competition inherent in these data driven materially based bureaucratic practices. Again, like bureaucracy, competition is a value generated from the capitalist mode of production. This results in student alienation. They become alienated from other students, the work they perform, and the products they produce as well as alienation from their instructors, administrators, and the bureaucratic school system. Most significantly, they become alienated from themselves as creative social beings whose aim should be to work toward a transcendent sense of potential beyond the notions of "success" in the framework of capitalism. Finally, they become alienated by the overwhelming totality of the material structure in which they find themselves. While they may find a way in (inclusion), they may never find a way out.

It serves to stress the point that in an extremely general way words like positivity, growth, and success can be constructive words but, realistically, they are so embedded into the fabric of the capitalist mode of production and its ideological discourse that it would serve educators best to avoid these terms, let alone to avoid the overtly capitalist theories from which they are founded.

Educators would be far better off, in terms of cultural responsivity, if the work of late British Clinical Psychologist David Smail informed their pedagogy. His works *Power, Responsibility, and Freedom* and *The Origins of Unhappiness* provide a drastically different approach to understanding human psychology (in contrast to *Mindset! The New Psychology of Success!* [The title reads like an Edward Bernays advertising slogan]). He offers what he calls a Social Materialist approach to human wellbeing (or human mindsets). He asserts that the roots of mental distress can be found in our relationship within and to society as social beings. He offers ways to combat this distress through social means, outside of capitalist individualism and competition. One major aspect of his work that should be applied to pedagogy involves the indelible markers of class. Hammond barely mentions class in her text while she focuses, although vaguely, on ethnicity, race, and gender.

It would serve educators tremendously to understand how economic class informs the mindsets of students or to state it a different way, how the capitalist mode of production determines to a great extent the mindsets of students. The major divergence of Smail's claims to psychological claims that rest deeply within the ideology of capital involves navigating away from the intense focus on the individual mind or what Hammond could call: the pedagogy of solipsism. The capitalist mode of production and subsequent ideology has overwhelmed humans to the point that "We believe that happiness [or success] is obtained through personal development." To combat this conditioning to individualism "our only hope is to 'de-centre' ourselves, to see that we are not islands and that our existence does indeed make sense only as 'part of the main.' We are social creatures who have come to mistake our nature as isolated individuals."[11] Essentially, mindset theories push students into their own minds or into almost exclusively subjective ideas about the material or objective world. Each individual becomes the center of the universe. Their minds serve as the entire arena (or factory) to produce their successes (or failures). Therefore, all the responsibility to be successful lives in one place: the mind(set). But as long as there exists negative concrete economic (material) realities that shape the mind, students will never have the autonomy nor responsibility that is presupposed in idealist theories obsessed with the minds of individuals. Therefore, since most students fail (or do not achieve their dreams), most will interpret this failure as their own personal failure and, thus, will tend to avoid addressing the real source of their (so-called) failure: the failures of the capitalist society.

Mindfulness

Hammond also proposes mindfulness, a concept steeped in the idealism of the liberal middle class. It is widely reported how mindfulness has become a major facet of the self-help industry and has snuck its way into pedagogical practice. Again, like the individualized aspects of data collection and bureaucracy, mindfulness reflects the overemphasis on the experiences of and from the individual mind. Hammond's text looks at the individual mind of the educator as the vector to overcome things like implicit bias and micro-aggressions by understanding one's own cultural identity. It goes without saying that cultural identity emerges from capitalist material conditions that inform the ideological biases of individuals as well as the biases of the culture at large. The major mistake here is the presupposition that culture is an individual experience that can be overcome individually while still being embedded within capitalist material conditions and its culture. Mistakenly, Hammond offers a hyper-individualized solution to overcome biases through mindfulness.

Of course, in some circumstances, self-reflection may serve to potentially create breakthroughs in understanding ourselves individually, but two problems exist with this idea:

1) We self-reflect with the same cultural biases or ideological framework that we aim to overcome. Simply identifying it without changing the capitalist mode of production that informs it always results in the re-enforcement of the capitalist mode of production.

2) Mindfulness, as a commodity, is an intricate part of the very biases we aim to recognize and overcome. To put it simply, hyper-individualist thinking will not overcome hyper-individualist thinking, especially since it is framed within the confines of capitalist discourses of individual success, personal development, careerism, hierarchy, and bureaucracy.

Again, being aware of some things personally, and even changing those things we are aware of personally, does not change the dominant modes of cultural practice because the dominant modes of cultural practice in capitalism is individualist and emerges from the underlying mode of production that relegate humans to atomized automatons. Being the change we want to see in the world is an absolutely incorrect way of changing the world because change is not an individual experience based in ideas from the mind or in solipsistic (idealist) foundations. Rather, a change in the mode of production informs changes in cultural practice.

Hammond quotes from Neuropsychologist Rick Hanson's book *Hardwiring Happiness*, whose work offers some of the same commodified self-help jargon (veiled in neuroscience) that one might find in the early twentieth century work of Émile Coué. Hammond paraphrases Hanson by writing, "The key strategy of calming the lizard brain is to practice relaxation and mindfulness. So, start a meditation practice, take up yoga, or join a drumming circle."[12] The lizard brain does not think but reacts. So, to combat the lizard brain one needs to take time to relax and meditate and then one can rewire the brain to negate reptilian thinking. This sounds great, and the idea of meditating and playing drums seems relaxing and fun, but her recommendations and assumptions overlook two important factors:

1) If one has time to relax, meditate, take up yoga, or join a drum circle, then one is already in a position within capitalism to, at least temporarily, escape capitalist notions of time (productive labor and consumption). In other words, a certain range of economic security is necessary along with a certain range of preexisting mental health. As Smail's book *The Origins of Unhappiness,* in its profound case studies, clearly reports, social and material conditions generate mental distress that leave people without the mental health that would facilitate the ability to perform activities like meditation, yoga, and drum circles. Not to mention that the concrete financial circumstances displace the sort of "free time" that is also necessary. Occasionally deeply distressed individuals may use these activities to overcome their lizard brains, but again, a few individuals do not change the society

that causes the inflammation or triggering of the lizard brain to begin with.

2) Along with presupposing the economic security and mental health to meditate, do yoga, and play congas, Hammond, at least in this context, foregoes or overlooks the social-material aspect of these activities. Meditation and yoga might be done with a group of people. Drums circles must be done collectively. So, perhaps it isn't the meditation, yoga, or playing drums which quells the lizard brain, but rather the collective social activity, itself, that quells the lizard brain. Therefore, it is not an act of mindfulness at all, but rather, a social-material activity that generates, not just mental health, but good teaching methods, through activities of solidarity and collectivity. Conversely, if meditation and yoga are solely individualized subjective experiences, as they are promoted, then they do nothing to challenge the hyper-individualized principle of capitalism where self-reflection and mindfulness serve the central purpose of making an individual realize success within a capitalist economy and education system.

Keep in mind that growth mindset and mindfulness exist as part of a combinatorial marketing unit to "feel good" and "be the best versions of ourselves" because of the dictates of bureaucracy and the precarious nature of our employment. The very system that creates the problems offers the solutions (as commodities). It is an industry that has become highly developed and appears all over media. Coupling this self-help advertising with pedagogy fuels the industry as part of the greater culture that promotes hedonistic egoism, ethical solipsism, and narcissism and serve as the dominant cultural mores in capitalism. As Baudrillard notes, "to differentiate oneself is precisely to affiliate to a model . . . to a combinatorial pattern of fashion."[13] All of the aspects of "self-care" that permeate concepts of "growth mindset" and "mindfulness" present themselves as individual processes of wellbeing and conform to a combinatorial package of retail fashion under the guise of scientific mental health practice. The pseudo-science embedded within these practices is the same pseudo-science of gurus, mystics, herbalists, and any other new age marketing package. It should be troubling to consider that these sorts of ideas have entered into regular pedagogical material and practice. It should be obvious that the capitalist mode of production produces these ideas.

The central failure of these concepts involve the age-old truism of treating the symptom and not the cause. Students and educators live in a mentally ill world based in competitive material conditions that objectively cause mental distress. In order to keep the material structure of the system of capitalism in place (the cause), these methods of "self-care" must be mobilized to treat the symptoms. It is common to read or hear proponents of these methods state that in order to help others it is necessary to first help one's self. The problem lies in the fact that the helping of one's self will never end and thus the process of helping others will never begin. This is the case because the underlying cause of mental distress remains and, subsequently, the mental distress remains and, furthermore, self-care must continue infinitely. Again, the fact that this is capitalized upon in the market adds a troubling layer to the equation, but the fact that it enters pedagogy presents the most troubling aspect for students and educators.

Some of the major flaws of cultural responsivity overlap into other pedagogical frameworks under the central heading of diversity, multiculturalism, equity, and several other catch phrases that dominate the education of the liberal middle class, both in theory and practice. It is useless to critique conservative educational theory and practice (privatization, market driven, for-profit, Nationalistic, Christian, etc.) since it offers little hope to improve education and will objectively make things worse for most people. So, again, this critique serves to question the dominant assumptions about education from the liberal middle class. Overall, cultural responsivity essentially reinforces the capitalist status quo by propagating the major precepts of the capitalist mode of production. Its success and influence in educational circles could be a result of successful marketing and advertising, the general ignorance of educational professionals or, more cynically, an uncomfortable fact that liberal educators of the middle class support and aim to maintain capitalism while posturing for a better society.

Regardless, cultural responsivity should be discarded as quickly as possible.

---

[1]https://www.goldmansachs.com/our-firm/about-us/awards/diversity-awards.html, from their Awards and Ranking page.

[2] Jean Baudrillard, *Consumer Society*, 89.

[3] https://www.youtube.com/watch?v=Jz50_ee4EKg (4:38), from The Real News Network, May 18, 2015.

[4] Jean Baudrillard, *Simulacra and Simulation, 7.*

[5] Zaretta Hammond, *Cultural Responsivity*, 100-102.

[6] Michel Foucault, *Discipline and Punish*, 183.

[7] Mark Fisher, *Capitalist Realism*, 52.

[8] Hammond, *Cultural Responsivity*, 105.

[9] Hammond, *Cultural Responsivity*, 109.

[10] Ibid, 25.

[11] David Smail, *Power, Responsibility, and Freedom, 5.*

[12] Hammond, *Cultural Responsivity*, 54.

[13] Baudrillard, *Consumer Society*, 88.

Chapter 2: White Teachers & Multiracial Racial Students: Gary Howard Ignores Economic Class

Another problematic text that addresses notions of liberal middle-class idealism in education comes from Gary S. Howard entitled *We Can't Teach What we Don't Know: White Teachers, Multiracial Students*. Like Hammond's text, its rhetoric appears to offer a challenge to the conditions that underlie racial problems in capitalist society but fails to deviate in any substantial way from these underlying forces, specifically in altering how schools operate within capitalism to combat racism. The text mainly focuses on changing minds and not material conditions. The central claim is that White teachers must recognize their own racial advantages and then work to remove the internal biases that emerge from these racial advantages. Howard's text almost entirely ignores class structure, even as it relates to multiracial populations.

The text epitomizes a central and yet obvious problem in education. White people of the middle class disproportionately, due to class structure, have better access to higher education. Therefore, White people of the middle class dominate the professions in education. Moreover, this is the audience to which Howard writes his book. In fact, after reviewing many pedagogical texts, from bell hooks to Henry Giroux to Michael Apple to Joan Wink, the main audience are White educators of the middle class. Subsequently, White educators of the working class see this material as out of touch with their actually existing material conditions because they are critiqued for their racial advantages. Whereas, nonwhite people of the middle class interpret this material without reflecting on the advantages of their economic class, which is more aligned to educational practice rooted in the advantages of the White middle class. In short, White and nonwhite educators of the working class are more aligned with each other than with middle-class educators of their own respective races. This is something Howard avoids almost entirely in his book.

Howard, who incorporates his own narrative of traditional White classism accounts for his own advantages exclusively through the lens of race. Sometimes this is revealed, as with this anecdote:

> An African American colleague, who is dean of the graduate school at a large urban university, recounted such an experience at a recent workshop. He told of driving his new BMW through a White neighborhood and being stopped by a White police officer who confronted him with a question, "Where did you get this car?" My friend responded, "I bought it, and you can buy one, too, if you have enough money." . . . My colleague reflected on this experience: "No matter how many academic degrees I may have, and no matter how prestigious my position in the university may be, in this confrontation with the police, I was just one more suspicious Black male driving a fancy car through a White neighborhood. This cop made his

> feelings clear that I didn't belong in either that car or that neighborhood."[1]

If interpreted purely from a lens of race, an obvious act of insidious racial profiling by police is evident, but Howard should have unpacked the class dimension within the anecdote. For instance, in terms of appearance, only a certain class of White folks could have been "in that neighborhood" and only a certain class of White folks could "belong in that car." Most importantly, only a tiny fraction of White folks could afford to buy the car. As Adolph Reed Jr. explains, "if you look at how white and black wealth are distributed in the U.S., you see right away that the very idea of racial wealth is an empty one. The top 10 percent of white people have 75 percent of white wealth; the top 20 percent have virtually all of it. And the same is true for black wealth. The top 10 percent of black households hold 75 percent of black wealth."[2] The point Howard and others aim to make is that a White upper middle-class person would not have been harassed by a cop like his Black upper middle-class colleague. This is a valid argument, but it also highlights a complete disregard for classism or how class determines policing (and other aspects of life) within races.

Howard describes a moment where he could interrogate the "intersectionality" of the moment, but ignores the space where race and class meet. In other words, just as one can accuse Socialists or Marxists of "class reductionism," one can accuse Howard of race reductionism. Therein lies the problem of ignoring class when discussing race.

Clearly Howard's book focuses on race, so understandably, in this context, he ignores class, but the trend in educational circles of the liberal middle class is to preclude discussions of class structure. If, for instance, poverty becomes a topic, it generally revolves around racism as the cause of poverty. It rarely involves the fact of poverty inherent in the capitalist mode of production. Recall the volumes written by Marx and Engels that describe impoverished conditions of (White) working-class folks in 19th century England.

In Howard's anecdote, his African American colleague owns a *new* BMW. Therefore, his colleague makes a clear decision to identify with the middles classes and decides to display his upper middle-class status via an expensive consumer commodity. Undoubtedly both Howard and his Black colleague sit on the liberal end of the political spectrum, and this reveals the inadequacy of liberalism in fomenting the necessary structural changes to capitalism and its obsession with social injustice rather than economic injustice via capitalism. Therefore, the adherence of the liberal middle class to capitalism forces educators to focus on race because a focus on class contradicts their own economic and class position and contradicts the signs of class position as manifested in expensive consumer commodities. This factor makes Howard's anecdote baffling in the context of a book aware of economic antagonisms. His inability to see such a staggering example of class antagonism baffles.

It also alludes to the essential problem of focusing on race as a means to generate comprehensive structural change. The class position of his Black colleague points to the fact that a higher ratio of nonwhites in the middle class will not create a more overall equitable system. Instead, like the circumstances for all working-class folks, a few select individuals can enter the realm of "success" while the rest, structurally, cannot. Capitalists who allow more nonwhites into their ranks of technicians, managers, academics, and so forth still leave us with capitalists and the inherent antagonisms produced through the capitalist mode of production. This leads to further class antagonisms.

One important example comes from the city of Atlanta, GA. In 1974 Maynard Jackson, raised in a highly educated, middle-class family, became the first Black mayor of any major American southern city. As mayor, Jackson led one of the largest strike and union busting operations in the history of organized labor. During the Atlanta Sanitation Workers strike of 1977, Jackson fired over 900 workers. Neal Shirley and Saralee Stafford note that "middle-class Black organizations and churches remained steadfastly loyal . . . [to Jackson] . . . who passionately opposed the strike on budget grounds."[3] Like Howard's Black colleague who aimed to display his class status, Jackson displayed his class status by directly harming the Black working class.

Is this because Howard's Black colleague and Maynard Jackson are morally inept people? No. It is because in a capitalist system morality is foregrounded by the material conditions of productive activity. This is not to imply that there is some sort of virtue in people of the middle class who avoid displaying their class status with consumer commodities or who overtly avoid dominating the working class in some other dimension. This *is* to say that the material forces of capitalism require specific class behaviors from those who are of the middle class, just as capitalism requires specific class behaviors from those who are positioned in the working class. These requirements, via the objective material structure, transcend race. The point with Jackson is that he was Black, and *the budget* dictated his behavior toward Black workers.

Another all too common example comes from a middle school where the economic class distinction between Black administrators and teachers of the middle class conflict with Black parents and students of the working class, this common situation reinforces Reed Jr.'s comments on "intra-racial inequality."[4] One former teacher deeply familiar with school policies and practices notes that the economic class divide dominates the general operation of the school, which is made up of a 90% Black student population. Essentially, the Black administration and faculty operate upon a strategy of strong discipline. For example, teachers force their students to be absolutely silent in the classrooms, to silently walk in straight lines to change classrooms and to hold stacks of textbooks in the hallway as punishment for not being silent during class. Much of the time students sit and eat in silence during their lunch periods. The basic pedagogical outlook, based in discipline and policing, suggests that these working-class Black students must be policed. In essence, the school mirrors the policing policies and practices found in the community and in any given prison. The general practices within the school involve both constant discipline and constant record keeping and categorization as control mechanisms of class positioning.

Furthermore, constant micromanagement found in bureaucratic corporate enterprises govern administrative function and classroom practice. If one's classroom is too noisy administrators or other teachers feel compelled to visit the classroom to silence the students. This despite the fact that students may be working actively and collectively on classwork or projects. In addition, *every* teacher planning period includes teacher professional development, which usually comes from either the corporate sector, such as textbook publishers, technology peddlers, or promoters of some sort of "for sale" package as a school improvement strategy or revolves around discipline and religious-based motivational sermons.

The very common example from this middle school highlights the fact that race alone serves as an ineffective form of organizing to address economic insecurity because economic class distinctions exist overtly within racial communities and are manifest by the daily practice within schools where the great majority of the administration and faculty are of the middle class while parents and students are of the working class. Just as Howard's Black colleague reproduces the appearance of class status with a new BMW, educators at this middle school and countless other public schools reproduce the disciplinary culture found in the workplace and the social sphere within capitalist relations of production. In short, the practices of the administrators and faculty at this middle school underscore the classism that develops from the objective class structure inherent in capitalism.

Furthermore, one can look to President Barak Obama's policies and practice on immigration to explain how capitalism foregrounds how differing nonwhite races come into conflict with each other. Obama earned his nickname, "The Deporter in Chief" by "removing" millions of people during his presidency.[5] Obviously, everybody must advocate for the rights of migrants and undocumented workers, but it must be done alongside anti-capitalism because economic factors serve as the chief motivation for both migration and the policing of migration (not to mention the overt exploitation of migrant labor). The majority of those who claim asylum will enter for-profit detainment centers. Again, "the Obama administration attempted to tamp down the number of Central

American families seeking asylum in the US by keeping families in detention and processing and deporting them as quickly as possible."[6] So under Obama, profits were generated for detainment with subsequent removal. Both sectors of capitalism, profit and discipline, proliferated.

Aside from Obama's policies on immigration, "Latinos" make up the majority (51-52%) of Border Patrol Agents and one-fourth of ICE agents. The reason is evident, as Brittney Meija reports about Imperial County, California, "[Border Patrol] is a job in a county with the second-highest unemployment rate statewide at 17%. The Border Patrol is one of the top employers in Imperial County."[7] People need to work. They migrate to work. They police migration to work. Obama's policies correlate with these necessities under capitalist exploitation and its mode of production.

To reiterate the central point, unless the capitalist mode of production is challenged alongside racism, economic class will determine the decisions made by high-ranking nonwhite leaders and of nonwhite people of the middle class. Howard circulates around this point when he writes, "Today we see a more complex phenomenon, wherein families from all racial and ethnic backgrounds, once they have achieved a level of economic success, will follow the money to the suburbs or private schools, thus creating a green flight."[8] Whether it is Mayor Maynard Jackson, administrators and teachers in public schools, President Barack Obama, "Latino" Border Patrol and ICE agents:

class structure, much of the time, overwhelms race. The most disparaging fact in all of these examples is that class structure requires economically mandated policing, the very issue that confronted Howard's Black colleague with the new BMW. Whether Howard's Black colleague likes it or not, policing is required in order for him to maintain the benefits associated his upper middle-class status. The two cannot be structurally separated.

This supports Cornel West's claim that there are always two basic responses of the capitalist class: "Repression on the one hand, co-optation on the other. Kill them off or buy them off."[9] The above examples illustrate how once bought off, it becomes more or less a class requirement to support the policing that kills off. This does not mean that any person or people fail morally. Rather, the basic responses in capitalism emerge from the very structure of capitalism. Herein lies one of the core problems. Structurally, only so many people, regardless of race, can be bought off since only so many people can enter the middle class. Therefore, the great majority of people must be left out of the relative security, comfort, and success that the middle class find within capitalism. Those who are left out must survive. Moreover, many survive via black market capitalism (both nationally and internationally via drugs, guns, smuggling, and trafficking, etc.). Many emotionally survive via drug abuse (prescription drugs and otherwise), alcoholism, etc. Therefore, those who cannot be "bought off" must be policed and/or "killed off."

The Achievement Triangle: Dimensions of Knowing

Howard discusses something he calls "The Achievement Triangle: Dimensions of Knowing" and prefaces his discussion with the following:

> The process of growth toward transformationist White identity requires the acquisition of many new ways of knowing. For those of us who choose to teach in racially diverse schools, this knowing comprises at least four arenas: that race matters, that change begins with us, that beliefs greatly influence outcomes, and that teaching is a calling, not just a job.[10]

Rhetorically, this excerpt epitomizes the general problem of how White liberal pedagogy from the middle class presupposes teaching practice. Howard falls into the solipsistic trap of starting from "I." "Ways of knowing" or questions of epistemology should not start with the subject, but rather with the material conditions which inform the development of the subject. From this starting point, the only place to go involves a change of "I" and not a change of the material conditions that result in the predictable formation of "I." "I" will (be)come what the material conditions produce. Second, Howard again gives too much autonomy to the subject when he notes that individuals "choose to teach in racially diverse schools." This might be accurate for White folks from the middle class, but for those from the working class, choices of where and whom to teach become material questions of necessity. For a White person of the working class, getting a job constitutes the breadth of the choice. Howard offers a general misunderstanding of economic realities, most likely informed by class status. Those from the working class fully understand that when it comes to work, choice is inherently limited and always insecure. Perhaps White teachers of the middle class "choose to teach in racially diverse schools," but teachers of the White working class apply for teaching jobs and simply hope to get one.

To return to the knowing, the first one states that "race matters." Of course race matters, but it does not matter in a vacuum. It matters in a concrete society where it intersects with material factors, such as political economy. To understand race means to understand that material conditions (or forces) in society inform subjective ideas about race. In essence, race becomes intimately intertwined with, among other things, political economy. For example, take the justifications of slavery. When notions of liberty conflicted with the economic necessity for cheap human labor, African slaves became defined as less than human. Therefore, race emerges, at least partly, from a material foundation that requires the necessity for low cost or free labor power. To reiterate, race exists within a society where it becomes manifested by the material forces of society that exist outside of personal subjective ideas about race. For example, the exploitation of African slaves problematizes subjective notions of race as the basic economic necessity resulted in Africans capturing and selling other Africans. For instance, in the country of Liberia many former slaves enslaved, captured, and sold other Africans as slaves on the legal and black markets.[11] Essentially, individual or even collective subjective ideas about race did little to combat the material economic forces that pushed former slaves into the act of enslaving. Therefore, race matters, but must be understood in the context of the material conditions that give rise to ideas about race. These material conditions are most obviously foregrounded by the capitalist mode of production. Howard keeps race in a vacuum and hopes that every individual will individually nurture and manifest the best possible ideas about race in their minds, despite the concrete material factors that inform ideas about race in society.

Howard next states that "change begins with us." Again, this statement places a vague group of individual subjects (White educators) at the center of change. Obviously, change must be collective, but in the context of "The Achievement Triangle," it mainly focuses on individuals who must aim to change themselves individually. The expression also serves as a somewhat hollow catch phrase that potentially can apply to anything in any context and to anybody. In fact, this constitutes one of the issues with the contemporary struggle for change: the repetition of vague and hollow phrases. Essentially, when the base of pedagogical theory rests upon ideology then ideological change emerges as the basic presupposition in pedagogical claims. Hence, change begins with ideological change and through ideological change comes structural change. The idea revolves around changing minds. Then, those minds will act and change structures.

The fact that there exists a base ideology, so to speak, that must be challenged and changed illustrates an ideological circle or trap. The presupposition assumes that White teachers and students enter the classroom with some distinct ideological base and that that ideological base includes unconscious biases and manifests in things like unconscious micro-aggressions. The counter presupposition assumes that students of color (and perhaps teachers) carry an ideological base that involves inadequacy, inferiority, and low expectations. The role of White teachers consists of recognizing their own ideological base and then changing it to avoid bias and micro-aggressions. Then, the teacher's ideological change results in a change in practice, which then initiates the ideological change in nonwhite students. Howard refers to this with the phrase: "beliefs greatly influence outcomes."[12] Notice how this reasoning never challenges the material structure of society that creates White bias and the concrete feelings of inadequacy of nonwhite students in the first place. These biases and inadequacies do not emerge solely from the mind. They have a specific material and, more significantly, economic base. Howard and the like focus on changing minds and not structures. Ultimately, the subsequent ideological base is capitalist, which is an ideological base that all people born into capitalism can identify with and, therefore, to some extent, transcends race.

Finally, Howard states that (White) teachers must feel that "teaching is a calling, not just a job."[13] The claim rests in the ideology of "teaching as a noble profession." The vision of the selfless teacher who spends countless hours meticulously reviewing student work, tutoring after school, paying for their own supplies, volunteering as club leaders, and so on, comes to mind. While this heartwarming vision ennobles the educator, it also conflicts with the brutish reality that teaching is a job. Regardless of how noble the teaching profession appears and how visions of selfless grandeur proliferate about teachers and teaching, teachers must teach for wages. But perhaps since Howard writes from the discourse of the liberal middle class to an audience of those of the liberal middle class, those of the White middle class who become teachers do not have to teach for wages to survive. Perhaps the "calling" comes from class privilege, e.g. you have been called from the comforts of your suburban security to teach students of color in impoverished and dangerous places as an immense sacrifice, from which you will be rewarded with the stamp of nobility. All of this presupposes infinite and eternal advantages for those of the White middle class and infinite and eternal impoverished and dangerous places populated by nonwhite folks of the working class. This is the ideological circle or trap.

Essentially, Howard points to the idealism of the inner subjective journey of White people of the middle class embedded within "The Achievement Triangle." The triangle, itself, includes three modes of internal (mindful) practice; 1) Knowing my practice. 2) Knowing my self [sic]. 3) Knowing my students. Again, notice the internal subjective or solipsistic nature of the triangle through the repetition of the pronoun "my." Educators, according to Howard, must reflect internally. For instance, he suggests that educators should carry a "highly complex set of professional knowledge, including curriculum, pedagogy, instructional design, developmental psychology, history and philosophy of education, legal issues, human relations, cross-cultural communication, and conflict management."[14] He personally notes that "The more I have examined my own [self-knowledge] related to race, culture, and difference, the less likely it is that I will consciously or unconsciously expose students to my own assumption of rightness, my luxury of ignorance, or my blind perception of the legacy of White privilege."[15] Therefore, Howard proposes comprehensive teacher education programs that prepare White teachers academically for their calling. Then, he shifts to the nurturing of the internal consciousness of each White teacher as a means to avoid exposing students to their White privilege. In reality, "The Achievement Triangle" becomes more like the Bermuda Triangle as a space where White liberal educators of the middle class can disappear into the ocean of their own minds as false consciousness.

Truthfully, nonwhite students of the working class can see the racial advantages of the White middle class even when White middle-class teachers go to great lengths to hide these advantages. Moreover, people of the working class of all races always see the class advantages of people of the middle class of all races. Although not addressing education, Mark Fisher adds some context to this idea when he writes, "[British Clinical Psychologist David] Smail describes how the marks of class are designed to be indelible. For those who from birth are taught to think of themselves as lesser, the acquisition of qualifications or wealth will seldom be sufficient to erase, either in their own minds or in the minds of others, the primordial sense of worthlessness that marks them so early in life."[16] What Howard fails to recognize is that the indelible marker of class works both ways. White people of the middle class carry their indelible marker of class or their class advantages. If Fisher's entire quote is altered to read, "For those who from birth are taught to think of themselves as better . . ." then the conclusion is obvious: the markers of class advantage emanate from people, including teachers. This also transcends race. So, without any clear objective strategy to challenge classism via a challenge to the capitalist mode of production, both comprehensive education and the nurturing of some internal subjective sensitivity will ultimately result in the eternal perpetuation of the class antagonisms, e.g. secure White teachers of the middle class and insecure nonwhite students from the working class.

Finally, Howard mentions that White teachers must know the "cultures, racial identities, languages, family backgrounds, home situations, learning characteristics, economic status, personalities, strengths and challenges, and uniqueness of each of our students."[17] To repeat, Howard espouses these practices as a vector toward the transformation of White identity and, eventually, teacher practice. Actual concrete material transformation does not exist in these practices. These are purely subjective internal transformations that *may result* in some sort of material change, but that is not Howard's central concern. If his premise involves White privilege and privileged White teachers must learn the cultures, racial identities etc. of the students, then the ideological circle or trap maintains its encirclement.

The central strategy to overcome the disconnect between White teachers and multiracial students must include objective and concrete changes to the entire economic system. Class antagonism is the disconnect, and it is compounded by the concrete iniquity of race. Racial division is not an internal reality based in subjective feelings. It is an external objective reality based in the material structure of society. Getting rid of unconscious bias in one's head through an education of racial populations does not alter the material realities of economic insecurity that nonwhite folks live within in objective material reality.

---

[1] Gary Howard, *We Can't Teach What we Don't Know: White Teachers, Multiracial Students*, 90-91.

[2] Adolph Reed Jr., Walter Benn Michaels "The Trouble with Disparity," Sept. 10, 2020, https://nonsite.org/the-trouble-with-disparity/

[3] Neal Shirley, Saralee Stafford, *Dixie Be Damned: 300 Years of Insurrection in the American South,* 194.

[4] See his article with Merlin Chowkwanyun entitled "Race, Class, Crisis: The Discourse Of Racial Disparity And Its Analytical Discontents." & his article with Walter Benn Michaels entitled "The Trouble with Disparity."

[5]https://www.migrationpolicy.org/article/obama-record-deportations-deporter-chief-or-not, from "The Obama Record on Deportations: Deporter in Chief or Not?," Jan. 26, 2017.

[6]https://www.vox.com/2018/6/21/17488458/obama-immigration-policy-family-separation-border, from "What Obama did with migrant families vs. what Trump is doing." Jan. 21, 2018.

[7]https://www.latimes.com/local/lanow/la-me-ln-citizens-academy-20180323-htmlstory.html, from "Many Latinos answer call of the Border Patrol in the age of Trump," April 23, 2018.

[8] Howard, *White Teachers, Multiracial Students*, 121.

[9] https://www.youtube.com/watch?v=Jz50_ee4EKg (4:35), from The Real News Network, May 18, 2015.

[10] Howard, *White Teachers, Multiracial Students*, 126.

[11] See *Another America: The Story of Liberia and the Former Slaves who Ruled It* by James Ciment.

[12] Howard, *White Teachers, Multiracial Students*, 126.

[13] Ibid., 126.

[14] Ibid., 126-127.

[15] Ibid., 127.

[16]https://theoccupiedtimes.org/?p=12841, from "Good for Nothing," Mar, 19, 2014.

[17] Howard, *White Teacher, Multiracial Students*, 127.

Chapter 3: bell hooks: Teaching to Transgress & Teaching for Community

bell hooks offers a comprehensive description of the many issues surrounding race and class (and occasionally gender) in her text *Where We Stand: Class Matters.*[1] In fact, despite her popularity among liberal educators, her engagement with the intersection of race and class would surprise and may even dismay many liberals. For example, those White liberal educators of the middle class who find it easy to support anti-racism and gender freedom movements may find it difficult to embrace hooks' (somewhat) anti-capitalist and (tentative) pro-communalism stances. In fact hooks identifies this:

> Many folks with economic privilege who remain silent about economic injustice are silent because they do not want to interrogate where they stand. Sadly, all too often they stand in a place that is hypocritical. To challenge racism or sexism or both without linking these systems to economic structures of exploitation and our collective participation in the upholding and maintenance of such structures . . . [.][2]

hooks also adds to this a critique of the Black middle class, when she writes, "Significantly, even though a growing majority of privileged-class Black folks condemn and betray the Black poor and underclass, they avoid critique and confrontation themselves by not focusing on their class power."[3]

One of the most profound notions hooks advances involves the acknowledgement of White folks from the working class. She notes that most recipients of welfare are White[4] and composes an entire chapter about White poverty. She focuses on media representations of poverty that generate the perception that equates Black folks with poverty while ignoring or making invisible White poverty. This, subsequently, creates antagonisms within the working class that manifest in racism, as she mentions that this "allowed nonprogressive White folks of all classes to see themselves as the economic victims of needy Black folks stealing their resources."[5]

hooks also clearly indicates the limits of capitalism in terms of access to a job. She summarizes the movement for the inclusion of Black folks into the workforce and notes that "most Black folks naively believed that if racism and the job discrimination it condoned ended, there would be jobs for everyone."[6] Essentially, she clarifies the structural and material limitations of capitalism. Despite her extremely profound focus on the role of class structure as it intersects with race, she mainly offers an idealist critique that meanders through spaces like Christian morality, moralistic greed, consumer consciousness, ideological training through media, and other ideas in people's heads. This creates contradictions that never really address the underlying mode of capitalist production.

One example involves the contradiction with her claims about consumerism. While it is obvious that consumerist culture dominates the U.S. and, thus, Americans carry the minds of consumerists, the material structure of society informs these subjective ideas about consumer objects. Media certainly reinforces these ideas, so Americans cannot generate an alternative mindset. For example, hooks describes the near worship of consumer commodities that the youth display, but connects this to moral and idealist notions of greed and narcissism. Undoubtedly greed and narcissism prevail in a consumerist culture, but greed and narcissism *must* prevail in a consumerist culture when the underlying capitalist mode of production includes mandatory mass production (exertion/sale of labor power or necessary labor time) and mandatory mass consumption, (productive and individual consumption to guarantee the continuous and endless circulation of commodities).

Greed and narcissism penetrate the culture or *become* the ideology within capitalism, but the structural mode of production underlies this ideological dimension. It must. In effect, the words "greed" and "narcissism" can be avoided altogether in favor of the more objective term "capitalist." As a result of mandatory consumption, which is also social labor, consumerists must proliferate the society and inherently incorporate what appear as subjective impulses, e.g. the appearance of greed and narcissism. Objectively and by default every individual in the entire society is a consumerist and, thereby, to refer to individuals as greedy or narcissistic is redundant.

Similarly, poverty functions in much the same way as greed or narcissism, since it is built into the overall system or material structure of capitalism. Capitalism produces moral or ethical failures like greed and narcissism while it also produces concrete material failures like poverty. Poverty, furthermore, functions as a vector to moral and ethical failures as a presupposition toward more or less subjective feelings about the system that manifest in moral and ethical terms. Poverty works as a fail-safe all-inclusive path to evoke moral and ethical arguments that, moreover, evoke concepts of greed and narcissism. In other words, poverty is an outcome of greed and narcissism as well as an inherent part of the capitalist system. hooks repeatedly invokes the term "poor" and usually connects it to moral and ethical failures in society.

This presents problems for those who wish to combat the objective structure that objectively produces poverty. Slavoj Žižek cautions against this rhetorical and technical error when he asserts "I think we touch upon the central problem, which is that in this crisis [of capitalism] it is absolutely ridiculous to refer to some ethical values when it's the system itself in its normal function. [It is] the global capitalist system which is [always] pushing you towards violating some elementary ethical rules."[7] Of course, Marx makes this point throughout *Capital* and other writings and Jean

Baudrillard applies it to the *Consumer Society* when he writes, "If poverty . . . cannot be eliminated, this is because [it is] anywhere but in the poor neighborhoods. [It is] not in the slums or shanty-towns, but in the socio-economic structure." He continues, "Having said this, we should not believe that it is because they are deliberately bloodthirsty and odious that the industrial or capitalist systems continually regenerate poverty . . . Moralistic analysis . . . is always a mistake."[8]

hooks makes this mistake, possibly because of a basic misunderstanding of capitalism as a moral and/or ethical force instead of as material structure. She writes, "Yet this assault on the poor would not have been effective without the widespread embrace of hedonistic consumerism on the part of the poor."[9] As Baudrillard notes, there is no assault on the poor by bloodthirsty and odious capitalists, but rather it is, as Žižek notes, the normal functioning of the system. It may appear as an assault because the concrete signifiers of poverty appear (and are) objectively horrific. But again, it is an error to invoke an ethical or moral failure for the production and reproduction of poverty. Furthermore, "hedonistic consumption" also serves as an objective outcome (or consequence) of the normal function of the system (as well as crisis). Marx notes the necessity of individual consumption as simple reproduction. He notes:

> The fact that the worker performs acts of individual consumption in his own interest, and not to please the capitalist, is something entirely irrelevant to the

> matter. The consumption of food by a beast of burden does not become any less a necessary aspect of the production process because the beast enjoys what it eats.[10]

Labeling consumption "hedonistic" in a vast consumer society that requires individual consumption as intricate to the process of production and the reproduction of the worker grafts an ethical and moral layer on top of a material and structural pattern. It is irrelevant if consumption is hedonistic or altruistic; it is still consumption. Two very tangible dangers arise when hooks grafts morality on top of consumption. The first involves a diversion into a nostalgic past that always may or may not have happened, e.g. make the poor moral again. hooks' notes the communal aspect of the poor from previous times as she claims, "Among the poor, sharing could no longer be a core value when folks began to embrace notions of liberal individualism . . . [.]"[11] A closer examination yields the fact that sharing was more common in an earlier stage of capitalist development. The inevitable move toward mass consumption can easily be charted, especially in nations that jumped directly (by force) from subsistence and communal systems of economic organization into capitalist systems. It was not a matter of morality that people shared and lived communally in previous times or in some system of conscious noble values, but rather it was an outcome or a concrete manifestation of the economic organization of the time and space.

Surprisingly, hooks' solution to the problem of ending classism and its immoral offspring, hedonistic consumption, is extremely elementary. It is simply to consume less: "In order to end oppressive class hierarchy we must think against the grain. Resisting unnecessary consumerism, living simply, and abundantly sharing resources are the easiest ways to begin an economic shift that will ultimately create balance."[12] Again, this nostalgia for a time and space in a previous moment of capitalist development still leaves poverty in its place. It is simply: live simpler. It also risks noble-izing poverty.

This relates to the second tangible danger, which involves the interconnected aspect of the capitalist mode of production. Consuming less negatively affects the entire system. If people begin and sustain limited consumption to "create balance," the very system of consumption collapses along with all of the essential parts of production, such as jobs and so forth. Perhaps hooks wants the capitalist system to collapse in order to usher in a new economic system, but this doesn't appear to be the case because she suggests:

> Job sharing[13] where a living wage is paid to everyone is another crucial way to address both unemployment and the need to provide parents, female and male, more time to create positive home environments where they can parent effectively. Working to create electoral politics wherein as citizens we can vote for where we want our tax dollars to go, for education or military spending, for aid to the poor and disenfranchised. Many citizens of this nation would welcome the

> opportunity to pay their tax dollars for institutional services that redistribute wealth. Our interdependency and care for neighbors and strangers could be highlighted by programs that would allow those with materially plenty to economically support families in need and deduct this money from taxes. Ironically, one can deduct money sent to the poor in other countries but not if we give to those who are desperately needy where we live.

These suggestions defy the basic logic embedded in the capitalist mode of production. With limited consumption, comes fewer jobs (regardless of "job sharing" and the wage), limited tax revenues, limited wealth creation, and so forth. These suggestions also keep the existence of poverty as well as the individualized or atomized nuclear family structural unit in place. Moving money from one place to another while limiting the cycle of production / consumption is not only contradictory, but almost guarantees a resurgence of the reactionary forces of capitalist production, which inevitably grow from historically previous forms of limited production / consumption. In the end, all of this is based upon an ethical and moral injunction of consuming less, which brings all of this back to the individualism involved in consumer choice where each individual must make the ethical and moral choice of avoiding unnecessary consumption. Hence, the very classical liberal individualism hooks proclaims as a problem unsuspectingly lurks as part of the solution.

Teaching to Transgress and Teaching Community

bell hooks' widely read work on pedagogy informs much of the practice in liberal educational settings of the middle class. She emphasizes ethics, values, morality, spirituality, feelings, emotions, and, most significantly, individual subjective experience. In fact, she dominates her two most prominent books about pedagogy with first person narration of her own experiences (as does her book on class). Therefore, the very base of her pedagogical awareness lies in a clear privileging of subjective (her) experience. This is not to say that her texts lack some sense of objectivity. Rather, they privilege a method of inquiry or a methodology that relies heavily on personal subjective experience and from this methodological starting point emerges its obvious consequence (and limitation) that fits comfortably inside the discourse of capital: individualism.

It is not so much that her work is egocentric, but that her vision of what education is and what educators should be are founded upon the concept of the individual (individual educators and students) who should aim to think, feel, and reflect critically. She presupposes that individual educators and students possess at least some range of personal autonomy. The central problems in her writing about class also exist in her writing about education. Like her book on class, her work on pedagogy powerfully attacks the institutional and structural prejudices of patriarchy and White supremacy, but only offers solutions to these predicaments that remain in the realm of personal ethics, morals, and feelings. In other words, she aims to combat objective material problems with subjective ideal practices. When she tries to offer material solutions they remain firmly within the very material structure that she aims to challenge. So readers are left with the subjective task of self-reflection that results in an inquisition of the self.

For example, hooks claims that educators and students must mutually regard one another as whole human beings. A whole human being is one who unites the mind, body, and spirit. Therefore, the ideal classroom would consist of individuals who have, at some point, united their bodies, minds, and spirits. *Teaching to Transgress*, published in 1994, highlights Zaretta Hammond's *Cultural Responsivity* could assert (almost thirty years later) that solutions to objective material problems could be generated through personal subjective mindfulness. Could educators logically view themselves as material beings living in a material world, within objective reality, and aim to change that objective reality through equally objective means? Or should educators' journey through the pathways of Westernized Buddhist[14] practices that rely on faith in ambiguous notions like the unity of the mind, body, and spirit? Obviously, these two options do not exhaust the potential attitudes of educators and the subsequent possibilities for change, and some good can come from a combination of objective and subjective understandings (which strictly speaking must happen), but it seems that the former would yield more tangible results.

But it is this emphasis on personal subjective experience and self-interrogation that underscores hooks' claims about pedagogy. Of course, she recognizes this criticism and responds by writing, "Many times people will say to me that I seem to be suggesting that it is enough for individuals to change how they think . . . [but they do not understand] how a change in attitude can be significant for colonized/oppressed people."[15] Then hooks describes the necessity for practice through Paulo Freire's concept of "praxis." Further she writes, "It always astounds me when progressive people act as though it is somehow a naïve moral position to believe that our lives must be a living example of our politics."[16] Aside from what appears to be a straw man argument, hooks does not offer much in the way of concrete strategies that would provide educators with the basis for transformative practice. Her claims hinge on the internal and personal changes of individuals (educators and students) and not on concrete material changes of society. While personal subjective changes do contribute to concrete changes in the objective material structure of society, a better strategy for educators would be to teach why and how to change the material structure of society (why and how to change things out there in society instead of things in their heads). This means that there must be a certain type of "politics." Perhaps the politics must go well beyond the limited horizon of the liberal middle class and must be radical. More significantly, this may illustrate the limits of hooks' own political horizon and the subsequent pedagogical practices that dominate the spaces in liberal education. If the politics, themselves, limit the horizon for change, then living these politics will mirror or manifest these limitations.

It is not so much that her position is naïve, it is that *it is moral*. Thus, it requires self-reflective transformed educators to teach a particular set of moral values to students who then must self-reflect and transform and then conform to that particular set of moral values. Additionally, the process of transformation involves continuous self-reflection to maintain the correct moral values, which parallels the continuous practice of meditation in Buddhism (or even Catholic confessionals). In simple terms, these pedagogical strategies contain the repressive moral structure of the major religions. If this is a pedagogy of liberation, as hooks calls it in Chapter 5, then it probably should not mirror the characteristics found in the hyper-religiosity of moral religious practice. This religiosity of social morality has played out in concepts like micro-aggression, where educators must self-interrogate their own unconscious acts of aggression in the classroom.

One example comes from her chapter on class in *Teaching to Transgress* where she offers literally no strategies for changing class structure with the exception of the internal subjective change that amounts to saying, "Stay true to your working-class roots" or "don't let them change who you are." Of course, this contradicts the well-established structural limitations set in place upon the movement into alternate economic contexts. If the range of behavior is limited for working-class folks in middle-class contexts and the success of working-class folk hinge upon conforming to the set of middle-class expectations, then working-class folks must conform. This does not signify a lack of moral character in the working-class person, which must be internally monitored, but rather it signifies the power of the concrete dictates of the material structure in an inherently classist society. Real survival is at stake for working-class folks. The aim to preserve the working-class mind in the middle-class context seems more difficult and less productive than changing the structure to eliminate class distinction altogether. Upon eliminating class structure, the conflict will no longer exist. Thus, working-class consciousness must be revolutionary.

One concrete strategy (or the merger of theory and practice) might revolve around the act of organizing for a revolutionary workplace. For example, a wildcat strike is a concrete material strategy (practice) that can potentially initiate material changes in the structure of the institution and society, at large. Educators can directly teach why and how to strike instead of trying to lead students in a process of transforming their minds and then acting in accordance with the ethics, morals, values, and feelings of the transformed mind. Something like exploitation of labor is not a state of mind; it is a concrete, eternal, and necessary part of the capitalist mode of production and should be taught as such.

Likewise, hooks tends to overestimate the value of subjective experiences. She devotes a chapter to essentialism and experience and mentions, "This pedagogical strategy is rooted in the assumption that we all bring to the classroom experiential knowledge, that this knowledge can indeed enhance our learning experience . . . [and] it helps to create a communal awareness of the diversity of our experiences."[17] The problem here is the assumption that there exists an actual or meaningful diversity of experiences. Part of the continuing neocolonial project involves homogenizing populations and diminishing diversity of experiences (cultural hegemony). This assumption comes from the privileging of subjective experience or the idea that each one's mind includes a unique self (or the conflation of the subject with the self). By overestimating individuality, hooks underestimates the objective material conditions that maneuver individuals into a material state of homogeneity.

The continuing obsession of the "I am" mindset complicates or even hides the fact that the "I" is an object or is objectified via modes of moral, ethical, and spiritual production (as well as consumer capitalist [re]production). The slide into moral territory is a slide into confusing the generally dominant dualism of the subject/object binary. hooks slides into this territory via a privileging of experiential knowledge. The subject and self are two different things, which she conflates and if the correct morality must be that of liberalism of the middle class, then the subject simply reflects as the subjective "I" only to objectify the separate self, e.g. "I recycle." "I am a recycler." "I [must] recycle because I am a recycler." Since subjects exist within a system that must objectify them, then a better strategy would be to alter how objectivity or the self as object can be transformed into a better object via a system of economic organization (perhaps a hidden and smoothly functioning bureaucracy?). So it is a matter of privileging a mode of thought about one's self *to* one's self. In simple terms, objectivity is inevitable, not only because of the structure of language but also because of the concrete material economic system. Therefore, to claim that the mass of objectified individuals experience a diversity of experiences as independent subjects is to contradict any argument about the more obvious nature of individual experience as objects.

In a very practical way, this can be observed and understood. The great majority of educators and students have been systematically homogenized in a consumer capitalist culture (materially, then ideologically). Their experiences are virtually the same and are housed within the consumer capitalist range of allowable experiences. Regardless of race, gender identity, religion, etc. every individual goes to the market (I am a shopper). Most individuals must sell their labor power (I am a worker). Every individual watches media and uses smartphones (I am a viewer and smartphoner). Every individual uses email and social media (I am an emailer and social mediaer). All of this is social labor that contributes to the circulation of commodities. These obligatory daily material practices highlight what is most dominant in the society. These experiences where individuals serve as maneuvered objects within the superstructure of consumer capitalism offer the most accurate understanding of how individuals live, what individuals do, and who individuals are. In fact, the range of experiences might differ on some sort of spectrum, but the goal of consumer capitalism, as a force that keeps moving by its own logic and reproduction, involves an inevitable narrowing of the range of experiences. This narrowing exists and can be empirically understood in very basic ways and cannot be combatted by substituting consumerism and capitalism with moral, ethical, and spiritual modes of objectification. In both scenarios, objectification remains. The question then remains: Is the moral, ethical, and spiritual object better than the consumer capitalist object? It seems that hooks' argument is a merger of the two or that humans can live morally, ethically, and spiritually within a tempered version of consumer capitalism, and that this can be achieved, pedagogically, through the sharing of experiential knowledge.

But this does not get humans out of the problem of objectification inside an objective system that inherently objectifies. Regardless, to return to more practical matters of pedagogy, hooks makes several apt points in her chapter on class in *Teaching to Transgress.* One, which gets to the heart of class antagonism in education, is: "If we trust the demographics, we must assume that the academy will be full of students from diverse classes, and that more of our students than ever before will be from poor and working-class backgrounds. This change will not be reflected in the class backgrounds of professors."[18] To support this claim, a professor on a hiring committee almost proudly confessed, "We will not consider any applicant who hasn't at least received their PhD from the best public university in the entire state." This professor essentially announced to a class of graduate students that they would not even consider a graduate of the very university, in which he was a professor and they were the students. In this case, only an applicant from the best public university would even be considered for the faculty position. Even worse he further confessed that "We will probably hire someone from a top ten private university like USC or NYU. We hope someone from one of those type of schools applies for the faculty position." As hooks eloquently reveals, there may be a diversity in class status among students, but there will not be a diversity of class status among professors. This is for obvious economic reasons.

Unfortunately, hooks fails to offer a concrete guide for transforming a classroom to alter or challenge class distinctions. She remains very vague on the issue by referring to "bourgeois decorum" and more discouragingly offers to give voice to those of privileged class status within the classroom. She writes, "One semester, a number of Black female students from working-class backgrounds attended a course I taught on African American women writers. They arrived hoping I would use my professional power to decenter the voices of privileged White students in nonconstructive ways so that those students would experience what it is like to be an outsider."[19] It seems very contradictory to speak against "bourgeois decorum" and then allude to protecting that very decorum by only using "constructive" ways to decenter voice of privilege. What are constructive ways? They appear to be the very decorum she questions earlier. Regardless, it appears that the best strategy would be to do exactly what the Black female working-class students expected and not only "decenter" the voices of White students of the middle class but also overtly and concretely speak against their voices (and their class status). This sort of pedagogical approach seems necessary, especially since there are so few of us from the working class in college and university classrooms.

This gets back to hooks' experiential knowledge. Obviously, if we trust the demographics, classrooms in many spaces will be full of bourgeois students of the middle class. Why should the experiential knowledge of the bourgeois and middle class proliferate in the classroom? The experiences of the bourgeois and middle class exist everywhere and flourish on full display (as the spectacle) in a consumer capitalist society, or the experiences of the working class are on full display as mediated through the gaze of the bourgeoisie and middle class (in other words, more bourgeois and middle-class perspectives).

Aside from the problems of experiential knowledge from the bourgeois and middle class comes the problems of the experiential knowledge of the racist, the homophobic, the police, and so on. All of these voices should be marginalized in a classroom of and for the working class. If educators allow for these voices in the classroom, it should only be to overtly and concretely teach against these voices. In the case of the privileged voices of the bourgeois and middle class, educators run the risk of sentimentalizing or emotionalizing (or legitimizing) their voices, which runs the risk of turning into compassion (albeit superficial) for those of the class of exploiters. This sentimentality and emotionality may reinforce the ignorant mantra of the bourgeois and middle class: "We are all the same." Objectively, in terms of economic class and all of the antagonisms that come with it, we are not all the same. Truthfully, this is the most important distinction between individuals (and groups), class distinction, because the way in which we are all the same (as objects of obligatory production and consumption) benefits one class and proportionately harms the other.

Chapter 10 in *Teaching to Transgress* offers a long dialogue between hooks and Philosophy Professor Ron Scapp. During their dialogue they discuss several different aspects of teaching and learning, most of which revolves around the practice of sharing and listening in a community form. It addresses the teacher's role in things like student comfort, engagement, freedom, and subjectivity. One particularly noteworthy aspect involves the relationship of their observations about classroom practice and what Scapp calls, "Genuinely radical critical teachers."[20] This is noteworthy because none of their practices could be considered radical (without even considering what "genuinely" radical might constitute). For example, hooks cites "sitting in a circle" as a practice of "progressive teaching."[21] Herein lies the central issue with the entire text. hooks presents her material with rhetoric that appears radical but follows through with teaching practice that fits into basic politics of the liberal middle class. This can be confusing, especially for teachers who genuinely want to teach to transgress. Obviously, hooks wrote the book in the mid-1990s, and perhaps current normalized practice may have been transgressive practice back then.

But this is not the case. Even if the practices hooks suggests in 1994 were considered transgressive in 1994, the suggestions simply are not transgressive, let alone genuinely radical. Since 1994, the opposite perspective has emerged. hooks' text appears more radical because the trend toward more conservative pedagogical approaches have emerged in educational circles of the middle class. For instance, Zaretta Hammond regurgitates hooks' ideas about mindfulness that directly correlates with capital and more profoundly highlights individualism. The trend toward sanitizing works like *Teaching to Transgress*, which were not transgressive in the first place, brings educators to texts and practices that are objectively more conservative than ever before.

This mainly occurs at the level of rhetoric. A term like "Cultural Responsivity" sounds transgressive. Intuitively educators think "I want to be responsive to the cultures of others" or something similar. But upon close review of the concept of cultural responsivity, one sees that it rests deeply inside the confines of capitalism, and not just any form of capitalism, but the harshest form yet, neoliberal capitalism. This unacknowledged or unperceived movement to the political right of liberal educators of the middle class epitomizes the most dangerous part of our predicament, e.g. we are not even aware of the movement to the right. Genuinely radical critical teachers, as the term implies, should probably be revolutionaries. Is there anything more genuinely radical than the aim to participate in and generate a revolution (an actual revolution, like the type Engels describes in *On Authority*[22])?

Regardless, another text from hooks, *Teaching Community*, discusses pedagogy. In the preface, hooks proclaims that we need mass-based political movements "to work for justice, changing our educational system so that schooling is not the site where students are indoctrinated to support imperialist White-supremacist capitalist patriarchy and any ideology, but rather where they learn to open their minds, to engage in rigorous study and to think critically."[23] Again, rhetorically this reads as a powerful statement against existing schooling norms and practices as well as inspirational goals for the future, but like *Teaching to Transgress*, the overall text fails to support this fiery rhetoric.

More importantly, upon close inspection, these ideas have problems. The first problem revolves around school as *the* site. Schooling is *a* site within a broad economic and cultural framework. School as "the site of indoctrination" carries further problems. To invoke indoctrination is to invoke something separate from the broad economic and cultural framework of any society. While it may be true that schools are sites of indoctrination, the problem with invoking it as part of an argument, means that the argument must pinpoint the school as a space of specific indoctrination while implying that spaces exist outside of indoctrination even though the school exists within an entire material framework where the same specific ideology grows. The school is not the site of indoctrination. The school is a site that structurally conforms to the dictates of the general material structure or the capitalist mode of production outside of the school, but more accurately, school is a site that is intricately connected to the economic framework of any given society.

Students do not enter a different space when they enter a school. The expectation that the school should be a space that functions differently than the space outside of the school appears objectively hopeless. Students exit one space of "indoctrination" (the world outside the school) when they walk into the school and enter another space with the same "indoctrination" (the school). Indoctrination becomes void because it implies that there is a specific ideology by specific entities that aim to take a student brain and shape and form it to their liking inside the school. This is not how ideology works. Ideology does not need a space separate from some other place. Ideology simply becomes part of the general experience of life. People live within very distinct forms of material organization. In the capitalist form, people must perform specific tasks in order to survive. By performing these specific tasks, people develop the brain (the emergence of ideology) that coincides with their specific function in the society. In capitalism, it is to work and consume. No specific indoctrination is necessary when in order to survive people must work and consume according to the normal function of the capitalist mode of production. School, as we know it, is simply the educational sector of capitalism. No separate ideological enterprise takes place. Therefore, educators cannot simply aim to change the minds of students against the so-called "indoctrination" at the school site. Educators must actually aim to change the obligatory functions for survival within the capitalist system in total, i.e. change the capitalist mode of production.

What happens when a student's brain is de-indoctrinated? The student then enters the workforce as what? How does the student carry on with consumption? The mode of production will still be in place upon de-indoctrination.

hooks' hope hinges upon the development of a mass-movement, and she seems to imply that critical educators can facilitate the educational part of the mass movement or even incite a mass movement through education. Yet, she states that students should not be indoctrinated by "any ideology." Is ideology not, at its most basic, the group of ideas that exist (or emerge) in any (and every) society? Can a society exist without ideology? This connects to hooks' ideas about opening students' minds to think critically.

It seems the line of reasoning follows a path from:

a. the student who does not have the opportunity to think critically to
b. the student who then has the opportunity to think critically to
c. the student who then thinks critically to
d. the student who then aims to reform the world to make it better.

There does not appear to be much more than this path. This is the horizon. It seems that the educator's role is to guide a student through a path that incites the student to think critically about the world they inhabit. This presupposes that the student, in the best case scenario, will discover, through critical thinking, the same vectors of exploitation and oppression that the educator believes to be exploitative and oppressive. In the case of students of the working class, this uncovering of exploitation and oppression via critical thinking will more likely result in mirroring the beliefs of the educators of the liberal middle class (or at least that is the hope or expectation). It might be different if the students come from middle, upper middle, or elite backgrounds. Regardless, there exists an underlying assumption or presupposition that information and self-realization (or self-actualization) through critical thinking leads to or connects to individuals who then work for changes in the world. This is almost an act of faith, and, nonetheless, still resides in the realm of ideology preconditioned by the capitalist mode of production. Except, through critical thinking, a substitute ideology may emerge. hooks claims that critical thinking can subvert indoctrination of "any ideology" without considering that the politics of the liberal middle class constitute the ideology she supports.

hooks implies that the consciousness of exploitation and oppression (exploitation-consciousness / oppression-consciousness) based on race, class, gender, etc. can emerge from critical thinking and then subsequently students will act to change the world and then the world can change for the better. In contrast, Marx describes consciousness, in terms of class (this can also be applied to race and gender), as a product or outcome of historical development. He writes, "with the accumulation of capital, the class struggle develops, and hence the class-consciousness of the workers as well."[24] Furthermore he writes, "The development of the contradictions of a given historical form of production is the only historical way in which it can be dissolved and then reconstructed on a basis."[25] The contradictions or antagonisms between classes allows consciousness to emerge as a product of historical development. This means that critical thinking imposes the emergence of a certain consciousness onto student minds, which basically negates critical thinking anyway. To think critically means that a variety of ideas might emerge from student minds. On the contrary, the goal of pedagogues from the liberal middle class, in the context of their politics, demands very specific ideas to emerge from student minds, e.g. liberal ideology and the virtual negation of critical thinking and emergence, in general. Obviously, the question must be asked: what if critical thinking results in the mass growth of ideas contrary to the expectations of pedagogues of the liberal middle class? This highlights the problems with critical thinking and the overall thread of reasoning hooks supports.

hooks later discusses teaching as a job. In a chapter entitled "Time Out," hooks asserts, "All teachers . . . need time away from teaching at some point in their career."[26] Another way to word it is "workers need time off work." The "profession" of teaching, especially for teachers of the working class, may have little to no job security, inconsistent benefits, varying wages, and so forth. So, teachers of the working class suffer from some of the same insecurities as jobs that clearly fit into what might be considered as traditionally working- class employment. Obviously, the past forty years includes the overt removal of job security, benefits, and the lowering of wages for almost all workers. This includes teachers. Therefore, to assert that teachers need time off conflicts with the necessity to work. hooks continues, "Certainly, the many unemployed teachers . . . could all work some of the time if teachers everywhere . . . were allowed to take *UNPAID* leaves whenever they desired."[27] This statement breathtakingly epitomizes labor consciousness among the pedagogues of the liberal middle class because it assumes that unemployed teachers could essentially serve as substitutes for a class of teachers on a higher level of the professional hierarchy. It also mentions unpaid time off! In order to take time off without pay, teachers must have money reserved. Without a doubt, some teachers save money and live a fairly comfortable middle-class life, but in terms of organizing labor within a broader movement of solidarity and rights, the notion of unpaid time off pulsates with absurdity. To be unemployed is unpaid time off. In higher education where tenured professors of the liberal middle class reside, their value can allow for this anti-labor perspective, but in the ordinary lower rungs where insecure teachers of the working class reside, this idea clearly benefits capital, which basically dictates school budgets. Imagine a working-class teacher approaching the school board to ask for unpaid time off with hundreds of thousands of unemployed teachers waiting for a job! The response from the school board:

> Take as much time off as you need, but we will have to give your job to someone else.

hooks acknowledges this later, "Even if college teachers had the opportunity to take unpaid leave . . . the vast majority do not have the economic means . . . to exploit this opportunity."[28] hooks does not follow this up with a discussion about labor organization for higher wages, etc. but rather enters a discussion about the individual subjective attitudes of teachers, e.g. they don't have time off, and so they have bad attitudes. Is this not the case with most work?

When we consider the predicament of working-class folks globally, much of "Time Off" reads like a fantasy. A subjective fantasy with ephemeral nods to personal responsibility and mindful self-obsession. When she addresses bad attitudes of teachers who suffer burnout, hooks quotes the self-help book for teachers, *The Courage to Teach*: "When I violate myself, I invariably end up violating the people I work with. How many teachers inflict their own pain on students, the pain that comes from doing what never was, or no longer is, their true work."[29] True work! In what economic position must an individual reside, in order to search for their true work? Is this not reserved for a certain class of people? What about coal miners? Or line cooks? Or migrant farm workers? Or debt collectors? Or paper pushers in cubicles? Or ride share drivers and so on? What if a book were written that told coal miners that coal mining is not your true work because you are burned out and have a bad attitude! Picture this: the coal miner explains how they can no longer face going down into the mine and breathe the dust and ash for twelve hours a day. They go home beaten and in despair. Their fellow coal miners, friends, and family all get violated when the miner inflicts their pain on all of them.

hooks points to an objective issue of poor working conditions and the necessity for individuals to sell their labor-power and offers an individual subjective solution to the problem. This keeps the poor working conditions in place. A teacher who successfully teaches without burnout and never develops a bad attitude is simply a teacher capable of silently dealing with poor working conditions and labor exploitation . . . because the working-class teacher needs the job to survive. The self-help internal coping mechanism may be called false consciousness, and the life of quiet desperation may be called bad faith, but regardless of the names, both strategies reinforce bourgeois and middle-class schooling and neither address the underlying problems of the teacher, especially the working-class teacher.

Turning away from working conditions and self-help, hooks explains why she uses the term "White supremacy." She notes, "I state my preference for using the word White supremacy to describe the system of race-based biases we live within because the term, more than racism, is inclusive of everyone. It encompasses Black people / people of color who have a racist mindset."[30] This presents a rather strange justification because the word "White" clearly indicates a specific race of people (regardless of social construction, etc.) and "supremacy" means what it means. The two words put together do not simply imply something about White people, but actually explicitly say something about White people, e.g. White people are supreme. The connotation extends to "White people are supreme and use their supremacy to oppress and exploit people of color." History shows that White people have certainly oppressed and exploited people who they did not consider White. Obviously, race gets complicated here because the vast history of White people exploiting and oppressing other White people serves as evidence that economic class must be considered in order to understand the entire scope of the issue. One can find this history in books written about primitive accumulation and industrialization in Europe where White on White exploitation and oppression is commonplace.

More obviously, there exists a distinct history of White people oppressing and exploiting nonwhite people through colonialism, slavery, and imperialism. All educators should know this information. Some don't. Some don't care. Others do. Regardless, the term "White supremacy" clearly uses the term White and, therefore, it seems strange to state that nonwhite people can be White supremacists. It certainly makes sense that nonwhite people can internalize the values of colonialism, imperialism, classism, and so forth, but perhaps a better name for this phenomenon would suit the discourse. The term "White supremacy" implicitly condemns all White people and implicitly offers nonwhite people the navigational mode to manifest all of the values of oppression and exploitation while maintaining a race based shield to avoid criticism for enacting these manifestations. This is incredibly evident in education. The other main problem revolves around the fact that most White people do not know about the social construction of race or critical race theory or any of the academic nuances that pertain to race based discourse. Countless poor Whites wonder where their supremacy exists and where their privilege lies. Again, obviously, simply having White skin certainly offers relative advantages. This cannot be denied, but when White folks who live in abject poverty surrounded by violence, drug addiction, and general hopelessness hear other people discuss their supremacy, it presents a massive disconnect and creates contempt.

hooks hints at this, but still prefers to use the term "White supremacy" because it includes nonwhite people. She continues, "Working-class Whites in our nation will often speak quite eloquently about the way racist assumptions fuel our perceptions and our actions daily, while White folks from privileged class backgrounds continue to do the dance of denial, pretending that shared class privileges mediate to transform race." This entire statement confuses her perspective because her explanation of the use of the term White supremacy "encompasses Black people / people of color who have a racist mindset." Who are these "Black people / people of color" who have racist mindsets? Do they share class privilege with White folks from privileged backgrounds? It seems by separating White folks from the working class from "privileged White folks" that hooks implies that same separation among nonwhite folks, e.g. division based in class status. Are those nonwhite people who internalize racism also those with privileged class backgrounds? If so, then class may actually mediate to transform race. All of the concepts that surround inclusion and equity always involve the idea of increasing opportunities for class mobility, i.e. shared class status.

The tension between her overt claims about racism with her tentative claims about class create this confusion throughout her work and make her preference for the term "White supremacy" problematic because White is White in the term "White supremacy." White is not working-class White and privileged-class White in the term "White supremacy," it is White. So, why make the distinction based in race when implying that the distinction is based in economic class? Perhaps working-class nonwhites take on the racist mindset of "White supremacy." If this is the case, how should this message be conveyed to the nonwhite working class? Should we tell nonwhites of the working class that they are White supremacists? In other words, the implication is that nonwhite people of the middle class are those who take on the mindset of "White supremacy." In that case, are they not simply people of privileged middle-class backgrounds?

The solution to all of this is that people "do their active unlearning of White-supremacist thinking by seeking to forge relationships with people of color."[31] This certainly makes sense, but like the choice to take unpaid time off from work or the choice to find one's true work, the time and resources necessary to make this effort exists outside of the narrow economic confines of the environments of the working class (or may already exist in that environment), and forging relationships with people of color exists outside of the general concern of the middle class. Also, if nonwhite people internalize White-supremacist mindsets, then is hooks saying that nonwhite people must seek to forge relationships with other nonwhite people in order to unlearn White-supremacy? Finally, hooks laments, "it was hard to accept being lumped, even if just for a moment, with all unenlightened White folks who have no intention of unlearning their racism."[32] It is certainly hard to accept being lumped with unenlightened White folks who have no intention of unlearning racism.

The last aspect of note in hooks' *Teaching Community* points to a specific structural problem within educational institutions. It involves the educational workers who generally get work within these institutions and why these particular educational workers get work. hooks writes, "In our nation most colleges and universities are organized around the principles of dominant culture."[33] While this states the obvious, the problem lies in what constitutes dominant culture. hooks describes her concept of dominant culture as "imperialist White-supremacist capitalist patriarchy."[34] Essentially, imperialism emerges from capitalism and proto-capitalist and subsequent capitalist societies were generally patriarchal. Although, this does not explain the more nuanced understanding of working class versus middle class / bourgeois class differences in how patriarchy manifests. Without the inclusion of hierarchy as a structural fact of capitalism, one can misjudge the role all men play in capitalist society, e.g. that all men have power and privilege and that all women do not. One simply needs to read the role of working-class men during the 19th century in England to see that working-class men had no power in relation to bourgeois men while working-class women played an entirely different role than bourgeois women, but more importantly working-class gender dynamics were entirely different than what could be described by the term patriarchy. hooks acknowledges that men are also victims of patriarchy[35] and White-supremacy has already been discussed. The central point is that hooks conception of the dominant culture aims to squeeze in every aspect of domination by separating the forms by race, gender, and class. Her overall explanation in most of her work confuses these elements of domination in the vague phrase "dominant culture."

It is especially vital to be specific about what constitutes dominant culture when discussing educational institutions and practices. hooks claims, "Since dominator culture promotes and encourages competition, traditional academic settings are not usually locations where colleagues learn to trust one another and to work in mutual partnership."[36] She also claims, "Relationships between Black and White women are often charged by the dynamics of competition." Finally, hooks reinforces this when she asserts, "Competition in the classroom disrupts connection, making closeness between teacher and students [and student between student] impossible."[37] In hooks description of the dominant culture, capitalism stands out as the central factor underlying competition in these social and educational spaces. So, instead of simply using the phrase "dominant culture" to describe competition, she should use the phrase "capitalist culture" because dominant culture includes White-supremacy and patriarchy, which do not constitute the location of competition. The capitalist mode of production assumes competition. The social world that emerges from the capitalist mode of production necessarily includes and privileges competition. Colleagues and students at universities, and women of different races compete because the capitalist mode of production produces competitive social relations. hooks aims to explain this away by adding, "Whether or not that competition stems from a racialized [or gendered] base, it will ultimately manifest itself in a racialized [or gendered] response."[38] Perhaps hooks' is correct, but this does not account for the fact that competition must be everywhere in capitalism. How can one understand the role race or gender plays when people of the same race and gender must compete because capitalism requires such? At the risk of controversy, it seems that hooks reduces everything to race and/or gender, even when the clear cause of the problematic social issue lies in the objective capitalist mode of production. Simply inserting race and/or gender into the structural fact of competition does not make it so.

hooks prime example of grafting race and/or gender onto capitalist mores involves the hiring of educational workers. She writes:

> When the candidates [for a job in education] are individuals of color coming from working-class backgrounds they may not "fit" with the group norm. The perception that they will not fit may make them lose jobs for which they are eminently qualified. It is a fiction that when faced with excellent students and professors of color predominantly White faculties will

> affirm and reward brilliance. Time and time again I have witnessed faculties support folks of color that they deem not very smart but hard workers over individuals who are deep and excellent thinkers and scholars.[39]

Again, the problem she describes results from the structural basis of capitalism. The group norm always sits upon the foundation of the capitalist mode of production and always includes a class dimension. The class distinction in the atmosphere of educational professionalism and efficiency circulates through each process within this highly controlled and meticulously constructed environment. To "fit in" already implies a class preference that subtly manifests through a specific set of predetermined guidelines. One guarantees a position in the basement of the structure if one is too bright *and* from the working class, regardless of race. Race reinforces the guarantee but is not exclusive to the guarantee. Simply put, those who are too bright and of the working class will not get the jobs. Those who are too bright, of the working class, *and* nonwhite will also not get the jobs. But here the main factors are intelligence and class and not race.

Conversely, and to reinforce hooks' point, for those who are not *too* intelligent, the predetermined guidelines work in the other direction with middle-class mediocrity as the significant factor, regardless of race. The hiring criteria below goes from most likely to get a job to least likely to get a job (Note: There are also circumstances of cronyism [friends, colleagues, same alma mater, etc.], nepotism [family], and tokenism [race & gender]:

1. Mediocre, middle class.
2. Mediocre, working class.
3. Excellent, working class.

Again, this rests upon a very clear part of the foundation of capitalism as Michel Luc Bellemare notes:

> Within the obdurate corridors of the post-industrial, technocratic, military-industrial complex, the best and brightest do not necessarily rise, within capitalist hierarchies, due to the fact that the best and brightest of the workforce/population, by definition are unique, moral, creative, independent, and thus difficult to classify. They are different from the bourgeois-capitalist status quo, automatically, making these segments of the workforce/population suspicious and questionable in relation to the mechanical workings of bourgeois-state-capitalism. [. . .] Subsequently, in order to curtail the independence and the deviations of the workforce/population, the logic of capitalism has prompted the industrialization and the militarization of education and society, in general, along the lines of mediocre bourgeois status quo. [. . .] As a result, there is a rampant development of a clear and definitive, capitalist set of pedagogic hierarchies, emphasizing bourgeois mediocrity.[40]

Moreover, hooks misplaces her critique. It should be a critique of the capitalist structure or the logic of capitalism and not of race. Race certainly exacerbates the situation, but the real foundation to the ascension of mediocrity in educational hierarchies comes from the tightly constructed and reinforced inclusion practices that preference and privilege mediocrity of the bourgeois and middle class as the number one criterion for advancement. Countless hiring committees that include mediocre faculty and administrators from all races almost always decide to include the most mediocre, neutralized, standardized, basic, generic, homogenized, conformist individuals of the bourgeois and middle class into the hierarchal realms of educational institutions across populations, regions, races, and so forth.

So to "fit in" always refers to class distinction and antagonism because those who are eminently qualified are disqualified because of their eminent qualifications, coupled with their class position, because those who are eminently qualified who come from the middles classes (which is a de facto eminent qualification, due to the access to the upper realms of educational hierarchies, e.g. attending and connecting with and in highly ranked universities, etc.), can "fit in" and will "fit in" because of their class and the dominance of individuals from those classes already operating and maintaining the educational hierarchy in the service of capital.

The preference for mediocrity could not be more evident by the near worship of Zaretta Hammond's incredibly mediocre text previously mentioned. The fact that large swathes of educated professionals view the content of her book as a vital and significant contribution to the field of pedagogy serves as the ultimate tribute the culture of capitalist, bourgeois, middle-class mediocrity. hooks is absolutely correct about mediocrity but misplaces her critique.

Overall, hooks' pedagogical texts avoid a critique that includes the impact of the mode of capitalist production and its inherent class antagonisms on educational practice and institutions. Her emphasis on reformism, individualism, and spirituality as well as her inability to connect class and race results in texts that more or less support the politics and ideology of the liberal middle class.

---

[1] bell hooks, *Where We Stand: Class Matters.*

[2] Ibid., 161.

[3] Ibid., 98.

[4] Ibid., 124.

[5] Ibid., 124.

[6] Ibid., 123.

[7] https://www.youtube.com/watch?v=Gw8LPn4irao (6:13-6:55), from Lecture: *Living in the End Times According to Slavoj Žižek*, Mar 11, 2010.

[8] Baudrillard, *Consumer Society*, 56.

[9] hooks, *Where We Stand*, 124.

[10] Marx, *Capital Volume 1*, 718.

[11] hooks, *Where We Stand*, 124.

[12] Ibid., 162.

[13]Marx already addresses the structural impossibility of this suggestion in *Capital Volume 1*, Chapter 25, Section 3.

[14] hooks cites Buddhist monk Thich Nhat Hanh as a great teacher of hers on page 56 of *Teaching to Transgress*.

[15] hooks, *Teaching to Transgress*, 47.

[16] Ibid., 48.

[17] Ibid., 84.
[18] Ibid., 189.
[19] Ibid., 188.
[20] Ibid., 154.
[21] Ibid., 146.
[22]https://www.marxists.org/archive/marx/works/1872/10/authority.htm, from "On Authority" by Frederick Engels, 1872.
[23] bell hooks, *Teaching Community*, xiii.
[24] Marx, *Capital Volume 1*, 808.
[25] Ibid., 619.
[26] hooks, *Teaching Community*, 14.
[27] Ibid., 14.
[28] Ibid., 14.
[29] Ibid., 15.
[30] Ibid., 28.
[31] Ibid., 36.
[32] Ibid., 60.
[33] Ibid., 130.
[34] Ibid., xiii
[35]https://imaginenoborders.org/pdf/zines/UnderstandingPatriarchy.pdf, from "Understanding Patriarchy," by bell hooks, 2004.
[36] hooks, *Teaching Community*, 75.
[37] Ibid., 130-131.
[38] Ibid., 61.
[39] Ibid., 89.
[40] Michel Luc Bellemare, *The Logic of Structural-Anarchism Versus the Logic of Capitalism*, 34.

Chapter 4: Toolboxes, Social Justice, & Ideological Clarity: A Cross-section of Liberal Middle-Class Pedagogical Failure

The mediocrity of the middle class plays a key role in hiring practices and, subsequently, the pedagogical practices implemented by mediocre hires. One example of this fact comes from a teaching manual called *OUR READING TOOLBOX: The Reading/Writing-Thinking Connection.*[1] The book includes a series of lessons that appear suited for elementary level students but was presented at conferences for college educators. The advertising summary of the book states, "*OUR READING TOOLBOX* will create a "Culture of Thinking" in your classroom. A close review of the text reveals that its structure actively discourages critical thinking. In order for critical thinking to emerge from the structural constraints of the lessons, the educator must provide a wide variety of texts and practices to compliment the lessons in the book. Above all, the text illustrates a dramatic example of mediocrity that can only yield, at the very least, bored students, and at the very most, entirely discouraged students. Its design appears suited for students who previously found little success in school, in terms of grades and so forth. So why it is promoted to college instructors for use with college students?

First of all, the academic conference presentation packet promoting the book and practices includes a section called "12 Strategies for Teaching & Learning."[2] Some strategies read:

Discussion-Oriented Student Seating Strategy

Arrange your students' seating in such a way that the students can comfortably see, hear, and communicate with each other across the classroom.

Name Tents and Randomly Assigned Seating Strategy

Use a "Name Tent" for each of your students so you can call each one by name from the first time you see them, and seat them randomly every class session.

Use of Speakers Voice Strategy

Explain to your students that each time they speak, they should use a strong, clear voice that can heard by everyone in the classroom.

Zenergy Chime Signal Strategy

Signal your class using a Zenergy Chime to capture their attention when a new phase of an activity is about to begin.

Collaborative Activities Strategy

Cultivate thoughtful discussion by having groups of two or more students work together to discuss and evaluate thoughts which they have written independently, prior to getting together.

Obviously, these strategies seem fairly basic and standard for just about any classroom. Things like speaking loud and clear, working in groups, timing assignments, using each other's names, and so on, all involve the basic functions of a classroom anywhere at any time. The surprising aspect comes when administrative and educational professionals present this information to a group of other administrative and educational professionals at professional teaching conferences, one of which that specifically addresses *college teaching pedagogy*. Who are the college teachers who do not know that students should be able to hear and see each other? Where are the college instructors who do not know that it might be helpful for students to work with each other and know each other's names? What college instructors lack concepts of time? Either way this entire feedback loop from college professionals to other college professions strongly suggests the mediocrity of all parties that emerges from the liberal middle class. Perhaps administrators and fulltime faculty (dominated by those of the middle class) who observe, evaluate, rate, and police other faculty (also dominated by those of the middle class) consistently see an utter lack of competence that inspires them to promote the most elementary and basic of strategies. This, in light of the fact, that both the administrators and fulltime faculty do the hiring! The incompetent teacher did not just appear from the heavens and land in a classroom. Were there not any better qualified instructors? This whole thing reinforces hooks' claims about mediocrity, but goes beyond race and into the entire fabric of hierarchal capitalist schooling. Mediocrity reigns as it takes mediocrity to hire mediocrity in order to assist mediocrity with mediocre strategies in a system where mediocrity *is* the strategy and required for the maintenance and reinforcement of status quo most exemplified in the middle class. The final questions: how can students rise above this mediocrity? If they do rise above mediocrity, will they be overlooked for employment in the field of education?

Overall, and perversely, it is better for students to match the mediocrity of their instructors, and it is also better for instructors to match the mediocrity of their administrative and faculty superiors. The obscenity of this structure lies in the fact that mediocrity is proliferated throughout the middle class and that this internal structure in education will simply continue.

This all implies an underlying suspicion about the capacity of both educators and, more importantly, students. An overall air of disconnectedness from the potential of students foregrounds these strategies, particularly students of the working class. For example, the continuing disregard for the capacity and overall ability of the second language learner manifests in the elementary "toolbox" pedagogy. As noted, college level administrators and educators presented this method of teaching and learning to other college administrators and instructors at a conference for teacher practice. They also presented this method at the California Teaching English as a Second Language (CATESOL) conference. ESL students who enter college in the U.S., enter with a variety of academic backgrounds. It is not unusual for ESL students to have had professional careers and advanced degrees in their native country and language. The only thing they lack are the second language skills. The elementary method of "toolbox" pedagogy undermines the capacity of ESL students.

Furthermore, the main teaching strategies of "toolkit" pedagogy carry a strange tension between oversimplification and needless complexity. The reading toolbox includes several items, such as the "paraphrase tool," the "title/headline tool," the "significant sentence tool," and the "problem tool," and the "implications & consequences tool." Instructors supply students with the textbook, which includes fifteen lessons (to fit a college semester) each with a couple of very short readings and a series of questions for students to answer that relate to the readings. Each question tells students to go to their toolbox to respond. The readings are simple. The questions are simple. The constant reference to the toolbox gets complicated as students must continually refer to this separate set of tools and their explanations in order to answer the questions. This results in students who must constantly flip through pages to find tools in order to respond to questions. Nobody is exactly sure who designed this confusing method, but to quote Rodney Dangerfield from the film *Back to School*, "I can assure you it's not the Boy Scouts."

Again, the readings and questions are extraordinarily simple. The only way they might elicit critical thinking from students is if the instructor provides deeper engagement with the reading that goes well beyond the lesson from the textbook. Each question supplies a tiny space to provide an answer, which illustrates the kind of question / response rote learning style via the toolbox medium (although the instructions mention students can use additional paper). If instructors need to go way above and beyond the textbook in order to incite critical thinking, then why use the textbook in the first place? (Mediocrity?) Between working-class students who survived years of this question / answer paperwork style of teaching and "learning" practice (that probably generated a dislike for school) and second language learners whose capacity goes well above the simplistic content of the readings, questions, and overall elementary structure of the toolbox textbook, very few students will enthusiastically embrace this method. They may endure it, but will not embrace it.

The textbook includes a speech from labor rights activist César Chávez.[3] Simply put, the reading does not require any critical thinking. It simply makes very clear statements that can only yield one explanation. While this does not represent a bad teaching strategy, in itself, it conflicts with the stated goal of "creating critical thinking." In the short excerpt Chávez states, "Today, the majority of children in our public schools are minority and they are from poor and working-class families . . . If the majority of children in school were White and if they lived in affluent suburban communities, we wouldn't even be debating how much money to spend on education . . . We must say no to suspending Proposition 98." Because of the short length of the excerpt and its extremely simplified content, students have little choice but to think of racism and voting. Again, rote learning and direct use of propaganda to influence student minds is not necessarily negative if the aim is to entirely transform the capitalist mode of production. But the toolbox textbook does not aim for revolution. This is obvious when Chávez's central plan against racism is to vote, e.g. we can vote away problems. Therefore, the worst-case scenario exists with this textbook because it privileges both a rote learning structure through the use of propaganda and liberal voting practices of the middle class that remain firmly inside the realm mainstream capitalist politics. If educators utilize rote learning through propaganda it should be revolutionary. Either way, the structure of the textbook does not generate critical thinking in the same way that cable news "point / counterpoint" talk shows do not elicit critical debate. The structure makes it impossible.[4] The Chávez reading can only yield one conclusion. Again, if the instructor provides a vast amount of further readings and context to the toolbox textbook, then the toolbox textbook could be effective as a means to begin conversation and critical thinking and writing. But again, if an instructor has the ability, competency, and intelligence to produce a unit of study full of thought provoking and relevant texts and writing prompts to generate discussion and writing, why use the textbook?

Aside from all of this a further problem circulates around the toolbox textbook that is incredibly common in mediocre pedagogy of the liberal middle class: the medium of paperwork.[5] Marx refers to paperwork as "the bureaucratic medium."[6] Ben Kafka's book on paperwork discusses one of Marx's early articles where Marx examines paperwork as a medium, particularly in an appeal to the state by winemakers to request lower taxes. Kafka notes, "Their [the state bureaucrats'] reaction [to the winemakers] was not a reflection of carelessness or callousness, but a specific effect of the material and psychic realities of what Marx named 'the bureaucratic medium.'"[7] Kafka continues, "for Marx . . . we must always be suspicious of paperwork, not of each other's' motives, but of the medium as such."[8] Although very few connect the work of Marx to Marshall McLuhan who famously coined the term, "The Medium is the Message," there appears to be a very obvious connection.[9] Marx predates McLuhan in analyzing paperwork as a medium that leaves no part of humans untouched, e.g. materially and psychically. Unlike McLuhan, Marx did not engage in media theory as Kafka refers to the previously mentioned article as "the most radical and articulate theory of media in Marx's oeuvre."[10] Nonetheless, the point is clear: paperwork is a medium and to Marx it is the bureaucratic medium.

Further, if "the medium is the message" then mandating students to engage in tedious paperwork yields other deeper effects and potentially negative consequences. McLuhan asserts:

> All media work us over completely. They are so pervasive in their personal, political, economic, aesthetic, psychological, moral, ethical, and social consequences that they leave no part of us untouched, unaffected, unaltered. The medium is the massage. Any understanding of social and cultural change is impossible without a knowledge of the way media work as environments.[11]

To stress the points, the authors of the toolbox textbook are not consciously careless, callous, or devious, but rather, their book serves as a manifestation of their own complete absorption into bureaucratic environments that chiefly require paperwork. Their own material and psychic realities permeate their pedagogical perspective and subsequent publication. Paperwork works them over and then they work over students with paperwork. This occurs without conscious efforts. Rather, the requirements and obligations of professional roles within a bureaucratic material structure results, almost organically, in automatic perpetuation through (dis)placing the same requirements and obligations to students. Power, in general, disappears in any personal, individual, or immediate relational sense. Power only reinforces itself through structural inertia or reactions to environmental dictates. The professional administrators and educators who penned the toolbox textbook simply follow predetermined practices deeply embedded into bureaucratic environments and pass them on to students. In essence, this is the power of the middle class as a class of technicians who reinforce the more powerful bourgeois or capitalist class.

Marx's central point in his article about the winemakers and the state authorities' reveals that individuals or groups of individuals become adherents of bureaucratic processes through, in this case, the bureaucratic medium of paperwork. The authorities who must decide whether or not to lower the taxes of the winemakers must review data on top of policy on top of precedent on top of, etc. The process leaves little room for conscious purposeful action. Therefore, the medium is the message. The medium of paperwork fuels an environment of bureaucracy.

Conversely, the content is not the message. The medium overshadows the article about César Chávez with his description of racism and his appeals for people to vote. The inaction that the medium incites correlates with the inaction of voting to eliminate the structural conditions that create and reproduce racism, e.g. the capitalist mode of production. Sometimes the content conflicts with the medium, but in this case the impotence of Chávez's message to vote aligns perfectly with an impotent medium. Just as voting exists within the inertial process of stale bureaucratic environments and reproduction so does the pseudo-aim for critical thinking via an uncritical medium that does anything but incite critical thinking. The entire toolbox textbook features the tedium of paperwork, which prepares students for the narrow spectrum of possible middle-class professional activity in a capitalist system dominated by the officious, hierarchal, and legalistic domains in a process of constant reproduction. Therefore, individualist appeals to individual subjective minds (or ideological reeducation) of professional administrators and educators will not change modes of practice because the material structure of officious bureaucratic activity necessitates and reproduces behavioral adherence. In essence, the roles of administrators and educators are (become) objective practices with little room for deviation (conscious or unconscious). Education is (becomes) a system of producing and reproducing middle-class objects, whether administrators, educators, or students. Just as César Chávez became frozen, impotent, bureaucratized, and objectified within the structural domain of officious organized labor, so do administrators, educators, and students within the structural domain of officious organized education.

Ideological Clarity

Ideological clarity represents another of the many theoretical offshoots of critical pedagogy. Although the pedagogues who teach and publish material about ideological clarity may deny it, ideological clarity, in both theory and practice privileges idealism over materialism and individual human subjectivity over conditions of objective materiality. It also epitomizes one of the central problems with pedagogical theories proposed over the past thirty years or so: it offers no clear vision or definitive horizon for the future and if it does it is entirely limited by the lack of vision of the liberal middle class. All of the potential positive changes in society remain vague, lacking any sort of specificity. The equation implicit in notions of ideological clarity follow this order:

Transform educators→who transform students→who both transform the world.

The usual vague ideas of racial (and gender) equity, equality, and inclusion fill the literature on ideological clarity, but it features nothing specific about what constitutes an equitable society or what an equitable society looks like and it never comes close to challenging the capitalist mode of production. As usual with these sorts of theories, they conflate racial and economic problems with a heavy emphasis on race and an extremely limited emphasis on class, e.g. if you're a person of color, you're poor, and if you're poor, you're a person of color. They always present the data as evidence, but never interrogate the data with a critique of class, only as a critique of race.

As the term "ideological" denotes, ideas play the most significant role in the shaping of the individual and the society. Therefore, educators must come to grips with their own ideological biases and prejudices. After much self-reflection and exposure to the right kind of experiences and information, educators recognize and articulate their own deeply embedded ideology. The vague term "dominant" followed by words like culture, society, narratives, etc. features regularly in the material, like a boogeyman or a fetishistic object. The term "dominant" serves as a replacement for more specific terms, such as capitalism, exploitation of labor, private property ownership, etc. and for all its focus on "naming," it does not name capitalism as the central system or productive mode of exploitation. It does include the occasional reference to class. One of the frequently cited scholars (in fact, this specific quote is used in just about every article and book about ideological clarity), Lilia I. Bartolomé writes, "Ideological clarity is the process by which individuals struggle to identify and compare their own explanations of the existing economic and political hierarchy with the dominant society."[12]

Obviously, the term "individual" jumps out and connotes the privileging for internal subjective ideas, and along with the term "struggle" reinforces the internal effort each individual must undertake in order to eventually and successfully overcome the dominant ____________(fill in the blank). Therefore, the definition of ideological clarity already assumes a preference for individualism and the necessity of struggle. Both of these ideological assumptions emerge from capitalistic material conditions. The pedagogues who promote ideological clarity fail to notice this contradiction. One of the cornerstones of capitalism involves the privileging of the individual over the collective. One of the other cornerstones of capitalism involves individual struggles for a better individual life. So from the very beginning, ideological clarity aims to overcome the dominant blank through ideology most promoted by the dominant blank, i.e. life is an individual struggle.

The mysterious nature of ideology hidden within the deep recesses of the mind do not need to be so mysterious; they do not need to involve struggle; they can simply be taught as parts of objective reality. It really does not matter if any one individual uncovers their own ideological biases and prejudices. It should be obvious that all people born in a capitalist structure are capitalists by default. To explain this to prospective educators, current educators, and students should be as simple as explaining addition and subtraction or the law of gravity. It can go something like this, if taught in the discourse of ideology:

> From the day a baby is born in a capitalist space, it is sent thousands of messages to go to the market for food, clothing, toys, and everything else in the world. The market becomes a naturalized part of life or simply normal. The child not only learns that it is normal to go to a market to buy stuff, but the act of buying and consuming becomes normalized. In other words, every person is a capitalist by default. You, I, and everyone are consumer capitalists from birth. Because we are consumer capitalists, we approach every decision in life with this ideological bias. The way to test this is to imagine doing something outside of capitalist consumerism (or consumer capitalism), like imagine collective practice as the objective means

> of organizing society. The first thing that happens when one makes this suggestion are the countless ways and reasons that collective practice won't work.
>
> 1. Some people won't work as hard as others.
> 2. Some will take too much.
> 3. People are too selfish.
> 4. People are greedy.
> 5. People don't get along.
>
> Notice how all these things against collective practice are capitalist values: competition, getting rich, watching out for me and mine, do not trust thy neighbor, etc. These immediate deflections of a society based upon collective practice is the ideological bias already built into the human in 21st century America and other capitalist spaces.

To understand this seems easy. It does not involve deep introspection or self-reflection, since all educators objectively experience this material reality. Perhaps this constitutes one of the reasons why pedagogues who promote ideological clarity avoid the topic of capitalism.

Actually, the real goal of ideological clarity explicitly circulates around racial (and to a lesser extent, gender) ideologies. Since it stems from critical pedagogy, it mainly focuses on the pedagogy for the oppressed, and in this case, racial oppression. Therefore, ideological clarity mainly aims for White educators to uncover their own unconscious racism, then transform, and then teach oppressed populations accordingly. Like hooks' work, all of this admirable, but also like hooks' work the horizon for change is at best unclear and at worst extremely limited. While critical pedagogy in the late 1960s may have included a revolutionary dimension, the ideological clarity derivative of the 2020s simply and overtly eliminates the revolutionary dimension. Obviously, this correlates to the differences of the material conditions of the 1960s compared to the 2020s. For example, revolution and liberation movements proliferated around the globe in 1960s while neoliberal capitalism proliferates the globe in the 2020s.

Hence, pedagogues who promote ideological clarity in the 2020s see the world through neoliberal lenses where individualism constitutes material reality in the dominant blank along with the presupposed struggle. Struggle in the 1960s meant collective revolutionary struggle in the objective material world while struggle in the 2020s means individual struggle within the subject's mind. Consequently, pedagogues who promote ideological clarity miss one of the major factors within their own internal ideological preferences, and with all of the talk of "critical historical inquiry,"[13] they seem to miss these contradictions. This represents the crux of the problem with ideological clarity. It simply offers nothing revolutionary in terms of changing society. It is liberal reformism of the middle class *par excellence*, but ironically, it is unaware of its positioning in liberal middle class reformism, as Bartolomé, un-ironically, subtitles one of her articles "Radicalizing Prospective Teachers."[14] So for all of its emphasis on self-reflection, these pedagogues of the liberal middle class have yet to self-reflect enough to discover the contradiction between reformism and revolution.

The rest of the quote reads, ". . . to identify and compare their own explanations of the existing socioeconomic and political hierarchy with the dominant society." This part of Bartolomé's statement presupposes that individuals carry meaningful differences in their explanations of the existing socioeconomic and political hierarchy. This founds the most essential problem with theories that privilege individual subjective knowledge and experience. Ideological clarity revolves around the education of both educators and students, but the assumptions appear clear: White educators of the middle class, who make up the majority of educators, will discover that their own explanations match those of the dominant society, and so they must work to change these explanations to avoid bias and prejudice against everyone else as well as to resist and counter the bias and prejudice of the dominant society. Everyone else (nonwhite middle and upper class persons, too) will discover that their own explanations also match those of the dominant society and must work to change these explanations to resist and counter the bias and prejudice of the dominant society. In both cases and, in almost all cases, the ideology of the dominant society generally dominates the "individual explanations." In fact, if it were otherwise, the system of domination would not be functioning properly.

Moreover, the question arises: If all individuals must have, by default, the same explanations of the existing socioeconomic and political hierarchy with the dominant society, why must individuals discover and compare them? The assumption that all individuals will carry the same explanations of the existing socioeconomic and political hierarchy within the dominant society should be the starting point. Educators should assume that all of their middle-class students not only share the same perspective of the dominant society, but also engage in behaviors and practices that reinforce the dominant society. Thus, educators and students can avoid the privileging (or data mining) of individual subjective experience and knowledge in order to directly teach the specific practices that will change (overthrow) the existing dominant society (capitalism).

This is one way to look at the subjective perspectives and ideological clarity, but more nuanced perspectives exist when inserting certain types of diversity. For instance, a nonwhite student from the middle class will share the same economic ideological perspective as the White student of the middle class. In other words, the student will espouse support for the general structure of the capitalist mode of production and its ideological counterpart that includes meritocracy, hierarchies of wealth are natural, hard work equals success, and so on. The difference of race may surface, but because the underlying material and ideological notions of capitalism already foreground the student's perspective, the racial difference will not result in the development of any radical economic change of the dominant society. Basically, the student of the middle class might reason: *the economic structure is not the problem. Racism is the problem. Racism prevents me from fully advancing in the economic structure. So we should keep the economic structure, but get rid of the racism. Then I can advance in the economic structure.* Moreover, nonwhite students of the middle class will not become anti-capitalists from being in classrooms with educators who teach ideological clarity. Also, the pedagogues of the middle class who promote ideological clarity were never anti-capitalist to begin with and, therefore, promote a pedagogy that will never be anti-capitalist. To repeat, the central aim of ideological clarity involves reforms for inclusion into the capitalist system and keeps capitalism firmly in place.

Conversely, the nonwhite (and White) students of the working class may have perspectives that intuitively counter the capitalist mode of production, e.g. hard work does not equal success, economic opportunities do not exist, and so on. These students may carry the indelible marker of class, which results from capitalist material conditions. Here, race can be coupled with class to radicalize students to change the dominant society because students of color from the working class already have tendencies toward anti-capitalism. But again, ideological clarity will not ignite anti-capitalist perspectives because it is not built to do that. It is not within its pedagogical structure and almost purposefully keeps anti-capitalism out of its rhetoric by proposing only vague and limited visions of change. In fact, educators who employ ideological clarity with students of color of the working class may do more to avoid changing the dominant society because of their narrow focus on racial explanations of problems coupled with reformist aims to combat these problems. This leaves the most potentially radical sector of the student population with incomplete data about their own oppression and even more incomplete data on what to change and how to change the dominant society. Obviously, educators must teach to examine and fight racial oppression and racism, in general, but it must be coupled with anti-capitalism and must be more than reformist.

One article that proclaims the success of a specific teacher (Carlos) because of a teacher preparation program that emphasizes ideological clarity illustrates the sanitized character of potential change and highlights the limited horizon for change within the pedagogical practices of ideological clarity.

Professor Cristina Alfaro describes the evolution of Carlos in her article, "Developing Ideological Clarity: One Teacher's Journey." While the article reads like a promotional piece for San Diego State's teacher preparation program, it also offers more than a glimpse into the low expectations of political and economic change. Alfaro describes her program and includes the usual and obligatory Bartolomé quotes, after which she explains how Carlos teaches indigenous folks in rural Mexico and then students in urban San Diego as part of his teaching preparation. She notes, "Prospective teachers begin to use their lived experiences to identify the linguistic, pedagogical, political, and ideological contradictions that exist in both the Mexican and U.S. educational systems."[15] To summarize, the contradictions involve race, ethnicity, and class, e.g. working-class and poor ethnic and racially marginalized students will receive a lesser and different education than students of different races and ethnicities of the middle class who are not marginalized in their local environments (what a discovery!).

It is important to contemplate how far outside of general economic, racial, and ethnic knowledge Carlos, and other students, must be *to not already know* these objective facts about education. This brings to light a truly frightening reality about who enters teacher preparation programs. Are those admitted into these programs so entrenched into their own middle-class ignorance that they have little to no knowledge about the objective facts of race and class within education? Furthermore, are they so ignorant that they must be flown to rural Mexico in order to discover these obvious objective facts? A sensible explanation involves the advantage of ignorance afforded to the middle class and the perpetual opportunities for these people to enter teacher preparation programs. This also gets to the underlying problem of ideological clarity. It seems to emanate from positions of economic class status. Seemingly sheltered young people of the middle class who are destined to go to college and who choose to teach must be shown the realities of those without class advantages in order to grasp their own deeply embedded ideological positions. In addition, Alfaro mentions that "Carlos came into the program with a predisposition (an open mind and heart) that allowed him to deconstruct, construct, and reconstruct his thinking about teaching and learning in a way that transformed him on a personal as well as a professional level."[16] Therefore, the aim of ideological clarity involves the transformation of students of the middle class (during the stage of teacher preparation), who have the correct predisposition, into teachers of the middle class who recognize their own advantages and, subsequently, lend a helping hand to those without these advantages. All of which fits into the matrix of liberal politics. Overall, in essence, this teacher preparation program includes a "slumming it" dimension.

Also, the separation between the personal and the professional bears significance. Again, this underlies and reinforces the logical problems at hand. Once the teacher enters into the professional aspect of the job, the teacher must conform to the dictates of the job. This can be understood in terms of context. For instance, at home, Carlos can focus on his *personal* state of being while in the classroom Carlos must focus on his *professional* state of being. The mandates at home differ from the mandates in the classroom, i.e. (potentially) human as *subject at home* and human as *object in the classroom*. But Alfaro suggests a subjective transformation through a change in objective conditions. Send prospective teachers to rural Mexico to teach marginalized indigenous populations and prospective teachers will transform as people and, eventually, as teachers. On the surface, this plan may look reasonable, but below the surface, it is illogical. When the teacher returns home from "slumming it" the objective material conditions or the context of the prospective teacher reverts back to the comforts and security of the middle class. Eventually, the advantages of these material conditions become heightened by the entrance into the security of tenured teaching with a consistent salary, benefits, retirement fund, etc. Carlos can live in objective comfort and security while the indigenous folks in Mexico still suffer. What is most important is that Carlos recognizes his own ideological position, which includes his own comfort and advantages. Hence, the short period of "slumming it" must have a long lasting affect and transcend the shift back to an objectively middle-class material environment.

This might appear as a moral condemnation of Carlos and all others who live in the security and comfort of the middle class, but this is a structural critique, not a moral critique. The central point revolves around the impossibility of the potential transformation that occurs via the use of ideological clarity as a means for change. The logical inconsistency appears obvious when understood through basic subjective/objective environments. Ideological clarity promotes an emphasis on subjective experience as a means to overcome objective conditions as exemplified in Carlos's overcoming of his own objective advantages through a previous subjective experience. Unfortunately, this hope falls objectively flat in the face of the evident conflict that emerges between Carlos's objective circumstances upon his return to the United States, such as the objective security of fulltime tenured track teaching employment versus the objective insecurity he witnesses (and "experiences") in rural Mexico. In both circumstances, Carlos's subjective experiences alter through his emersion in very specific objective material conditions. In simple terms, Carlos becomes his objective circumstances. If those objectives circumstances are secure, he becomes a secure person and ultimately loses any sort of subjective connection to the insecure objective circumstances of the indigenous in rural Mexico.

How do pedagogues who promote ideological clarity deal with this contradiction? Basically, they embrace it. Carlos refers to an often cited quote from Paulo Freire. Alfaro paraphrases, "Carlos describes another result of having participated in the ITEP [International Teacher Training Program] program: learning how to keep 'one foot in' and 'one foot out' in order to become a strategic educator. Paulo Freire explains that for teachers to work effectively with subordinated student groups, they must learn to be strategic in order to keep their job while carrying out their revolution."[17] When a teacher keeps "one foot in" to keep a job the objective experience of the teacher moves along a spectrum of obligations to the school district. This encompasses the central problem with this strategy. The objective requirements within the teaching profession de-revolutionizes the teaching profession, regardless of one teacher's subjective idealism (or personally clear ideology). The strategy to embed a group of ideologically clear teachers inside of large hierarchal institutions of domination as a means of revolution lives on par with embedding communists posed as Democrats within the U.S. federal government. All teachers know the structural constraints placed upon their activities to keep their jobs, but more significantly the change of subjectivity will occur with the embedding into these objective material environments. Carlos (we assume) certainly does admirable work within the southern California community as a teacher, but his admission of his own limitations housed inside a narrative of success seems, at the very least, ignorant, and at the very worst, disingenuous.

The use of the word revolution in this context is breathtaking and directly displays the disconnect between the actually existing practices of administrators and teachers of the liberal middle class who promote and use ideological clarity with the concept of revolution and the practices necessary to achieve one. To elaborate, Marx writes, "Through this movement he acts upon external nature and changes it, and in this way he simultaneously changes his own nature."[18] The structure of hierarchal educational institutions consolidate previous changes or "acts upon nature" that manifest in the material conditions of any given educational institution. Upon entrance into this previously constructed institution, all of the institutional practices change the nature of the human who enters. Just as the entrance of Carlos into the rural village in Mexico alters his nature, so does his entrance into the confines of a large bureaucratic hierarchical educational structure. Keeping "one foot out" does not combat the institutional obligations at the level of the individual subject and especially not at the level of the group and society.

This plays out in the near impotence of educators to change society (revolution) through administration and teaching. Things like paperwork, countless trainings, standardized curriculums, budgets, evaluations, observations, tedious lesson planning, meetings, and so on overwhelm any sort of revolutionary potential via "one foot in" and "one foot out" practices. This holds true at the level of the individual subject as well as at the level of any sort of collective subjectivity. In essence, educators becomes objects or are objectified ("changes his own nature") by objective material structures. Furthermore, although Alfaro does not mention it, the "one foot out" must always confront the necessity to have "one foot in." Educators do not leave the school and enter an autonomous zone of economic communism or anarchism. They enter a zone of hyper-capitalism that demands the same sort of daily practices that the educational institution demands. This makes the "one foot out" almost entirely an individualized subjective experience. Essentially, this is what ideological clarity is: an individualized subjective state of mind. Carlos summarizes the horizon for change in his owns words, which epitomize the limitations and contradictions of ideological clarity as a useful pedagogical strategy:

> First of all, to get it right, as in tenure, I must be very well informed of all the content area standards, and the California Standards for the Teaching Profession, por que aquí es todo lo que les importa [because here that is all that matters]. But, you and I know that it goes way beyond the standards with my students and the space of freedom I have created in my teaching, I bring in their reality. I have come to see their reality as my own! Students need to understand sus condiciones [their conditions], and, most importantly, what they can do to change their position of low status.

The changes never go beyond inclusion and upward mobility within the capitalist system. Talk of revolution serves as, more or less, hollow rhetoric when in actual practice the horizon for change falls inside the matrix of inclusion and the American Dream or in the reformism of the liberal middle class. All in all, those within educational institutions who have the security of fulltime tenure track work are the administrators and educators of the liberal middle class who represent the central promoters and proponents of ideological clarity. In the end, revolution would result in their loss of this objective security. Their positioning within the structure guarantees that this pedagogy will remain a harmless liberal set of middle-class practices housed within disconnected rhetoric about revolutionary change.

---

[1]https://titles.cognella.com/our-reading-toolbox-9781516507696#

[2] Conference presentation at CATESOL 2019 & Southwestern College Community of Practice Conference 2019.

[3] See the reading here: *The Words of César Chávez,* Texas A&M University Press, 150-151.

[4] See Noam Chomsky on concision.

[5] See the book *The Demon of Writing: Powers and Failures of Paperwork* by Ben Kafka, published on April 14, 2020.

[6]https://marxists.architexturez.net/archive/marx/works/1843/01/15.htm, Karl Marx, "Justification of the Correspondent from the Mosel," *Rheinische Zeitung* No. 15, January 15, 1843.

[7] Kafka, *Demon of Writing*, 114.

[8] Ibid., 118.

[9] Paul Grosswiler comprehensively connects Marx to McLuhan in his book *Method is the Message: Rethinking McLuhan through Critical Theory*. He writes, "The purpose of this book is to reconcile McLuhan and Marxism in order to contribute to the history of critical communication research, including qualitative and Marxist-based research. By illustrating the methodological foundation shared by McLuhan and Marxism, McLuhan's media theories may find a home in Marxist-based research and cultural studies (3).

[10] Kafka, *Demon of Writing*, 113.

[11] Marshall McLuhan, *The Medium is the Massage*, 26.

[12] L. I. Bartolome, "Critical Pedagogy and Teacher Education: Radicalizing Prospective Teachers." *Teacher Education Quarterly*, 98.

[13] See the article: "Critical Historical Inquiry: The intersection of Ideological Clarity and Pedagogical Content Knowledge" by Brooke Blevins, Kevin Magill, Cinthia Salinas.

[14] Bartolome, "Critical Pedagogy and Teacher Education."

[15] Cristina Alfaro, "Developing Ideological Clarity: One Teacher's Journey" *Counterpoints* Vol. 319, p. 231-249.

[16] Ibid., 236.

[17] Ibid., 244.

[18] Marx, *Capital Volume 1*, 283.

Chapter 5: Paulo Freire: Critical Pedagogy, Rhetoric, & Power[1]

Paulo Freire's powerful text, *Pedagogy of the Oppressed*, still stands as a testament to the spirit of revolution and liberation of the now distant 1960s. The overwhelming problems with the text prove evident in the pedagogy of the liberal middle class popularized in educational theory and practice. Freire's writing includes countless assertions that allow for it to easily conform to capitalism and its ideology. His material follows alongside the advancement of capitalism, particularly in its neoliberal form. This allows for the proliferation of Freire's ideas, through the analysis, interpretation, and practices of liberal educators and pedagogues, to reinforce neoliberal capitalism. To put it simply, the more neoliberal capitalism dominates and structures society, the more educational institutions become institutions of neoliberal capitalism. The more educational institutions become institutions of neoliberal capitalism, the more Freire's ideas conform to ideas of neoliberal capitalism. Unlike Marx, for example, whose ideas cannot, by definition, conform to the ideas of neoliberal capitalism, Freire's ideas can and do. This aligns with the neoliberal capitalistic practices of liberal educators of the middle class who, perhaps unsuspectingly, promote Freire's neoliberal biases.

Freire's work has been criticized for decades and covers a vast array of problems in his writing. Critiques include everything from his writing style to his sexism to his various contradictions and everything in between and date from the early 1970s to today. Three particular problems in Freire's work stand out as they relate to the specific failures that directly result in the content and popularity of liberal middle-class pedagogical texts. Without these original errors in Freire's work and his widespread fame, liberal educators and pedagogues of the middle class might not be able to harmoniously and simultaneously proclaim support for both liberation from the dominant power and conformity with the dominant power. The three particular problems involve his emphasis on individual subjectivity, his vague rhetoric, and his assumption of the power of educators.

Moreover, Freire fails to embrace any social, political, or economic theory that is explicitly against capitalism, despite employing some of the rhetoric.[2] Also, according to Blanca Facundo, "The United States context is simply too different from that in which Freire developed his ideas, and we have not really tried to explore the differences. It was easier to assume that the Third World was the same in any country."[3] Facundo's apt claim highlights an important consideration when critiquing Freire. In short, regardless of the context in which Freire developed his ideas, his claims to advocate or inspire some sort of liberation or revolution fail and, in fact, end up supporting the very dominant power he aimed to rally against in both the Unites States (First World) and the Third World.

Another significant point involves the fact that, to quote Baudrillard (while commenting on the post-revolutionary spirit and the failures of the left that manifested in the 1980s in the United States), "This is America's problem and, through America, it has become the whole world's problem."[4] As neoliberal capitalism transforms the entire world into satellite versions of the United States (economically, socially, culturally, etc.), Freire's original context becomes less and less of a factor. For example, something like the emphasis on individuality promoted through neoliberalism and inherent in the capitalist mode of production becomes simply part of global reality, thereby, blurring conflictual differences between the United States and the Third World.

Finally, a neatly packaged individualized form of colonialism gives people of the United States the opportunity to claim an internal subjective colonization of the mind or a Third World mindset amidst the advanced aspects of American society. Therefore, individuals can be Third World or colonized even while fully embedded in the United States. This subjective colonialism or colonial mentality serves as a means to posture as Third World residents in a First World nation and, thus, utilize Freire's theories, despite objectively living with all of the advantages of middle-class life in the U.S.[5]

Freire's Emphasis on Individual Subjectivity

Freire's emphasis on individual subjectivity, which includes self-reflection, critical thinking, and his emphasis on experiential knowledge, when encircled by the material structure and subsequent values of neoliberal capitalism, results in the seamless merger of the two, perhaps formerly, oppositional frameworks. For example, he writes, "Self-sufficiency is incompatible with dialogue. Men and women who lack humility (or have lost it) cannot come to the people, cannot be their partners in naming the world. Someone who cannot acknowledge himself to be as mortal as everyone else still has a long way to go before he can reach the point of encounter."[6] Like his offshoots, Freire uses language that reads and sounds radical, liberatory, and even logical, but under examination falters. One glaring contradiction involves "self-sufficiency" with what amounts to self-reflection. The question arises: If self-sufficiency is incompatible with dialogue, then why does dialogue require the previous (and even ongoing) step of intense self-reflection? This places educators into the circumstance of constant self-reflection to assure, subjectively, that they carry feelings of humility, mortality, equity, and so on.

Therefore, all of the prerequisites to name the world with students through dialogue always necessitates an inner subjective voyage of individuals. The "self" always precedes the other and the collective as the source of privilege. Nothing situates more comfortably into neoliberal capitalism than this mode of ideologically driven self-reflection. Some questions each individual educator must ask through this strategy are: Am I humble enough? Am I mortal enough? Am I empathetic enough? Am I loving enough? All of these questions must be asked while maintaining a distance from "self-sufficiency." This places extreme pressure upon the individual and as Walker explains, "We are not only moving in a circle, we are trapped in it. The tighter it gets, the more like puritanism and the less like liberation our new position will seem."[7] Is this not the predicament of the twenty-first century in neoliberal capitalism? The constant highlighting of individual subjective feelings with the hyper-emphasis on social correctness in every circumstance, not only in the educator-student relationship, but also in every social relation that exists whether in the workplace, on social media, with neighbors, friends, family, or as consumers and workers? Each and every moment must correlate to an object model of correctness that one can never fully and confidently manifest in each and every situation (i.e. the trap).

This represents the pedagogical version of the same solipsistic and narcissistic double bind, exacerbated by Freire's own injunction to sacrifice oneself, which permeates neoliberal capitalism. It results in a paradoxically subjective self-indulgent martyrdom. Again, Freire's focus on the self and individual subjectivity comes from a time when the dominant sources of power oppressively homogenized people and he speaks against this, but while dominant sources of power still homogenize people, individualism has evolved into the central tool of oppression in various spaces of neoliberal capitalism, such as in the self-love / self-help industries and on social media. Adam Curtis eloquently states, "What people suffer from is being trapped within themselves. In a world of individualism everyone is trapped within their own feelings, trapped within their own imaginations."[8] Freire's pedagogy reinforces this neoliberal capitalist entrapment within the confines of educational theory and practice, despite its call for liberation and freedom. Individual educators who trap themselves within self-reflective circuits cannot liberate themselves nor their students. Individual students trapped within self-reflective circuits cannot liberate themselves nor their educators.

Constant self-reflective circuits provide the liberal middle class the necessary narcissistic injunctions found in capitalist modes of social relation. They serve to produce a moral imperative or general contradictory morality that hyper-focuses on the self in order to help others, who simultaneously engage in their *own* hyper-focus on their *own* self in order to help others. In a strange paradoxical endeavor, self-help (supposedly) becomes collective help, but unlike in previous spaces of potential liberation, nothing exists that even remotely resembles a concrete horizon for collective and material liberation in the United States or any other Western Democracy (not to mention most of the rest of the world). Without the dimension of a collective and material liberatory horizon, the hyper-focus on the self reproduces both the material and ideological structures of the dominant power (neoliberal capitalism).

To further complicate his claims, Freire invokes several revolutionaries, including Amílcar Cabral, and the need for the middle class to commit class suicide.[9] He notes, "The revolutionary members of the middle class must be capable of committing suicide as a class in order to rise again as revolutionaries."[10] Donna Coben explains, "Class suicide is necessary because Freire assumes that the educator and the student come from different class backgrounds, but Freire's solution to this problem requires the teacher to sacrifice his or her class identity for the student."[11] Aside from the discussion on class status of educators and their students, the idea of any actions taken by a specific economic class, whether middle or working, sets up problems for individualism and the hyper-focus on the self. At what point do individual educators reflect upon their own middle-class advantages and then subsequently commit class suicide with other middle-class educators who also reflect upon their own middle-class advantages in order to later commit suicide as a class? This sort of solidarity and organization of the middle class, at the very least, needs a political party or some other central entity, which simply does not exist for educators of the middle class or people of the middle class, in general.

Regardless, the central point seems obvious: educators of the middle class will not commit class suicide via modes of self-reflection. A political party or some other use of force presents perhaps the only means to make this possible. In other words, educators of the middle class must self-reflect in accordance with mandates that require the middle class to "voluntarily" give up their advantages. Freire does not describe this scenario. Rather, his focus relies on each individual to self-reflect in order to come to class-based realizations about their own positions and subsequent actions. In all fairness, Freire writes this during a period of revolutionary fervor, which made the possibility of people from the middle class giving up their advantages a real possibility. As neoliberal capitalism continues to cover the globe in its image and reward the middle class for their subservience and class allegiance, claims of class suicide through self-reflective and later dialogical means appears completely absurd. As evidenced by the ideas of "ideological clarity" and students of the middle class who "slum it" with Mexican peasants, the students of the middle class do not even pretend to have the intent to commit class suicide.[12] Inevitably what unfolds with self-reflective pedagogy includes the same things that unfold with any individualized subjective (mindful) practice, a simulation of material change that coincides with a superficial set of ideological reinforcements.

This invariably runs into problems when the notion of "problem posing" content automatically reflects the problems posed by educators and pedagogues of the middle class. As John Berger powerfully maintains, "What happens out there happens to strangers whose fate is meant to be different from ours."[13] This provides the basic presupposition of the educators and pedagogues of the middle class. People of the working class exist as strangers whose entire range of experiences occur outside of the general embedded experiential knowledge of the middle class. The strangeness of contexts of the working class may generate sympathy among the middle class, but the structural constraints of educational bureaucracies and hierarchies prevents the middle class from activity that can tangibly alter the foundation of economic class structure or the capitalist mode of production. Therefore, class suicide requires an objective change in the material structure of educational systems and not an individualized subjective alteration of each middle-class mind. Berger's notion of fate aptly summarizes the predicament of the working class inside of a neoliberal capitalist system in motion that extends into educational institutions.

Freire's problem lies within the contradiction of individualism and collective class action. Essentially, he promotes class consciousness: one consciousness at a time. Not only is this inefficient, but it also relies on people of the middle class to become conscious of being of the middle class and then to consciously change their minds to the consciousness of the working class. Developing a working class consciousness does not occur like language learning via immersion. Rather, fate plays a key role and means that people are simply born into their class positions and from there, their class consciousness emerges. Students of the middle class may "slum it" and immerse themselves into contexts of the working class and may grow to understand and apply aspects of that context, but they cannot become working class. In truth, the class consciousness of the middle class serves as a default consciousness, which produces a continuous conflict within the consciousness of the working class. While an actual working-class culture may have existed as late as the 1980s, as is well documented in Jefferson Cowie's book *Stayin' Alive: The 1970s and the Last Days of the Working Class*, it no longer exists. The working class reside as a rhetorical ghost replaced by other less overtly economic identities like race and gender. While working-class culture no longer exists, working-class people continue to live within the confines of opioids, pollution, empty decaying homes, and rusted out factory buildings as essentially forgotten people.

While American cities all over the country decay, others have become large havens for the middle class who have displaced the working class. This adds to the disingenuousness of programs like the International Teacher Training Program at San Diego State University,[14] which ships students of the middle class off to far away zones of exotic impoverishment when the objective impoverishment of peoples in Gary, Indiana or Buffalo, New York could serve as apt locations to "slum it." Nothing exemplifies this situation more profoundly than the satirical song by the Dead Kennedy's called "Holiday in Cambodia," which describes the mindset of the middle class set against the atrocities of third world poverty and violence. The lyrics read:

> So, you've been to school for a year or two
> And you know you've seen it all
> Playing ethnicky jazz to parade your snazz
> On your five-grand stereo
> Braggin' that you know, how the n*****s feel cold
> And the slums got so much soul
> It's time to taste what you most fear
> Right Guard will not help you here
> Brace yourself, my dear
> Brace yourself, my dear
> It's a holiday in Cambodia
> It's tough, kid, but it's life
> Well, you'll work harder with a gun in your back
> For a bowl of rice a day
> Slave for soldiers till you starve
> Then your head is skewered on a stake
> And it's a holiday in Cambodia
> Where you'll do what you're told
> A holiday in Cambodia
> Where the slums got so much soul[15]

Again, Berger's notion of fate plays a key role in understanding the failure of individual subjectivity as a means for liberation from the dominant power, especially when coupled with class suicide. The fate of the working class determines their objective status as well as their consciousness. In a sense, Freire aims to alter the fate of the working class through altering the fate of the middle class. In the above lyrics, the middle-class student engages in the sort of artificial and consumerist practices of diversity training through exposure to "ethnicky jazz" and hollow conversations about racial poverty. Basically, the middle class temporarily enter extremely secure zones of impoverishment through officious means. The lyrics present the scenario of sending the middle-class liberal student to the harsh realities of Pol Pot's Cambodia to expose the superficial nature of the middle-class liberal engagement with the slums. The fate of Cambodians differs from the fate of middle-class San Diegans. The solutions to the problems of Cambodia (or Gary, Indiana and Buffalo, New York) do not and will not come from the middle class via their individualized, self-reflective practices and subsequent class suicide. Places like Gary, Indiana and Buffalo, New York might as well be as far away as Pol Pot's Cambodia, in both time and space, to the middle class. In fact, middle-class spaces in Gary, Indiana and Buffalo, New York might as well be as far away as Pol Pot's Cambodia (in time and space) to the working-class spaces in their own cities.

When people of the working class "swank it" and enter contexts of the middle class they may grow to understand and apply aspects of that context, but they cannot become middle class. Mark Fisher notes upon becoming a college teacher:

> I lacked the calm confidence of one born to the role. At some not very submerged level, I evidently still didn't believe that I was the kind of person who could do a job like teaching. But where did this belief come from? [...] the marks of class are designed to be indelible. For those who from birth are taught to think of themselves as lesser, the acquisition of qualifications or wealth will seldom be sufficient to erase, either in their own minds or in the minds of others, the primordial sense of worthlessness that marks them so early in life. Someone who moves out of the social sphere they are 'supposed' to occupy is always in danger of being overcome by feelings of vertigo, panic and horror.[16]

Freire and many of his eventual proponents fail to recognize, practice, or unironically articulate that the indelible marks of class work both ways. People of the middle class carry their own indelible marks of class. Rather than allowing for a counter-dialogue of working class (or peasantry based) analysis of middle-class contexts, Freire and his many eventual proponents carry their own markers of class when they promote the entrance of educators of the middle class into the contexts of the working class, as evidenced in Freire's work in Guinea-Bissau and the International Teacher Training Program at San Diego State University. In contrast, there exists no evidence of educators, administrators, or pedagogues of the middle class committing class suicide.

Imagine the moment when a middle-class educator asks a group of working-class students what can be done to solve the problem of poverty (problem posing) and the students point and reply: *You must commit class suicide!* Again, because middle-class consciousness serves as a default consciousness, folks of the working class live in a strange vertiginous hybrid zone of consciousness while people of the middle class do not. The material economic structure and the capitalist mode of production exists so that people of the middle class can simply choose their goals and work toward achieving them. This fact illustrates how self-reflective subjective activity emerges from the discourse of the middle class. If someone from the middle class does not fulfill their dreams, there must be something wrong with their internal subjective mindset or something is wrong on the inside. If someone from the working class does not fulfill their dreams there *is* something wrong in the objective economic structure of society or there *is* something wrong on the outside.

Therefore, the notion of subjective self-reflection rests comfortably inside the middle-class consciousness. The central obscenity of this sort of pedagogy is that it promotes this internal and subjective solution to folks of the working class whose issues are not exclusively in their heads but in their external objective material circumstances. Overall, Freire illustrates a sincere attempt, during revolutionary times, to construct an educational framework to come to the type of internal consciousness to foment various changes for the better. Unfortunately, as neoliberal capitalism spreads throughout the globe and firmly controls educators of the middle class, his work that supports individual means for objective liberatory change flounders, especially in the hands of the great majority of tenured educators and secure administrators of the middle class who will not even support their part-time and working-class colleagues (via union or any type of solidarity) for basic things like health insurance and guaranteed work (let alone to commit class suicide!). Perhaps the popular modes of internal subjective consciousness (growth mindset, responsibilization, mindfulness, meditation, self-care / self-love, etc.) provide a great deal of help for the bewildered brains of educators, administrators, and pedagogues of the middle class, but they serve little help to the concrete, material, and objective difficulties, of which the working class face. Within education in particular, it is easier to imagine the end of the world than it is to imagine educators, administrators, and pedagogues of the middle class fighting for health insurance and guaranteed work for part-time educators and educational support staff (let alone committing class suicide through self-reflection).

Freire's Vague Rhetoric

In addition, Freire's vague rhetoric about revolution, liberation, and change contributes to the similarly vague rhetorical notions of revolution, liberation, and change found in popular liberal pedagogy of the middle class. His vagueness leaves the space open for extremely harmless and saccharine "revolutionary" or "liberatory" aims. Furthermore, his goal to teach culturally different peasants the very literacy of the dominant colonizers expands the colonial project as much as the import of new technological objects or the mode of mass production from capitalism. Therefore, as seemingly revolutionary or liberatory Freire's work appears, it eventually produces a class of pedagogues, with corresponding theories, who comfortably integrate with the conventional routines of the capitalist educational establishment and who continue to perpetuate and support some of the characteristic elements of not only capitalism, but also neocolonialism and imperialism.

To be clear, Freire never engages in a critique of capitalism through his pedagogical theory. He was never an anti-capitalist. He uses the term capitalism occasionally, but does not commit to its overthrow. Furthermore, he substitutes very specific terms related to political economy like capitalism, bourgeois and proletariat for vague terms like the dominant class, oppressors and oppressed. Equally vague, his work includes the ultimate aim for humans to overcome dehumanization. Perhaps he utilizes these vague terms because of the potential of imprisonment, but his work in the 1990s, without fear of imprisonment, utilizes the same vague substitute terms.

The problem with these terms lies in their lack of specificity. Their lack of specificity allows for the possibility of anybody and anything to be classified as the dominant class, the oppressors, and the oppressed. In fact, the oppressors and the oppressed both constitute victims of dehumanization. Unfortunately, Freire privileges a subjective internal feeling or state of mind as representing dehumanization rather than dehumanization as a concrete, objective, and material fact. The oppressors are dehumanized at the level of their own psyches and so are the oppressed. Hence, if their psyches can be altered, they can become humanized. Ultimately, since Freire does not take a stance against capitalism and frames his work around vague notions of power, his work can fit into dimensions that support the values of capitalism, such as an emphasis on individual subjectivity. It also makes the enemy of the oppressed unclear. Who comprises the dominant class? Who oppresses? If Freire had used the terms capitalism, bourgeois and proletariat, all could easily identify the dominant class and oppressors, e.g. bourgeois capitalists. More importantly, all could easily identify a broader material economic structure of exploitation, e.g. the capitalist mode of production.

To be clear, Freire employs these various vague terms throughout the final chapter of *Pedagogy of the Oppressed*, but never offers any sort of picture of a post-revolution society aside from a general notion of humans who work toward humanization through dialogue and activity. Everything is always in some stage of dialogical process. He claims, "The taking of power constitutes only a decisive moment of the continuing revolutionary process."[17] Herein lies a problem that continues in educational practice of the liberal middle class: the endless process of revolution or dialogue. With this and Freire's continual focus on a cultural revolution, the problems compound into an ongoing and infinite process (what constitutes culture anyway?). At least to his credit, Freire uses the word revolution, even if it does not mean anything beyond a vague notion of humanization, and also to his credit he does quote, cite, and borrow from people who actually achieved revolution like Castro, Lenin, Che, and Mao, but as Freire's work moves through time to liberal pedagogues of the middle class, and as the really existing revolutions died somewhere in the process, the concept of "revolution as process" remains. The process, itself, can be anything that conforms to the existing order of neoliberal capitalism, but appears as and sounds like a resistance to it. Therefore, the emphasis on dichotomous dialogical relationships merging into a critically cohesive and transcendent humanity applies to any and every basic educational practice where, for example, teachers and students talk. Outside of education, one can look to the well-meaning but virtually impotent, Occupy movement to see this endless dialogical relationship in practice and in process.

In terms of revolution, Freire quotes, cites, and borrows from those who implemented material violence, but only mentions material violence in relation to the oppressors who commit violence on the oppressed. He goes so far as to state that (borrowing from and reframing Mao[18]), "Never in history has violence been initiated by the oppressed."[19] In other words, without a firm commitment to the actual material violence perpetrated by the revolutionaries he quotes, cites, and borrows from, Freire leaves revolution in an infinitely and firmly embedded state of conversational process. His notions about love and faith in people come directly from Mao, but unlike Mao, who saw fit to promote and execute a strategy of both violent revolution along with ideological training, Freire treads along the path of ideological training while simultaneously claiming that it is not ideological training (and leaves the violent revolution out of the equation, altogether). Rather, to Freire, ideological training or re-education, involves a faulty and deeply pseudo-complex dialogical relationship vailed in a transcendent humanism, i.e. we can all free each other through dialogue and become fully human. Overall, it results in an emphasis on idealist and cultural transformations without the "progressive war" Mao promotes and realizes, or to be clearer, the infinite subjective mythological, ideological, and cultural revolution without the finite objective, material, and structural revolution.

Furthermore, this lack of material change and privileging of ideological change comes from Freire's idea that "The internalization of the oppressor by the dominated consciousness of the peasants explains their fear and their inefficiency."[20] As long as the oppressor remains subjective, ideological, and possessive (like a ghost), liberal educators of the middle class can easily and forever aim to be exorcists. One striking comparison that exemplifies Freire's reframing of Mao (and other actual revolutionaries) involves the final chapter of *Pedagogy of the Oppressed* with Mao's *The Little Red Book.*[21] Freire does reference Mao during the chapter and focuses on Mao's expressions of cultural, ideological, and subjective transformations. The most interesting aspect of Freire's borrowing of Mao rests in Freire's omissions. For example, *The Little Red Book* begins with "The force at the core leading our cause forward is the Chinese Communist Party. The theoretical basis guiding our thinking is Marxism-Leninism."[22] Mao makes his politics very specific and very clear. He continues, "A well-disciplined Party armed with the theory of Marxism-Leninism, using the method of self-criticism and linked with the masses of the people . . . [.]"[23] This expression epitomizes the split between Mao and Freire. Freire omits Marxism-Leninism, but retains and repeats the concept of self-criticism. He reframes Mao's method of "self-criticism" as "critical reflection." He writes, "The insistence that the oppressed engage in reflection on their concrete situation is not a call to armchair revolution. On the contrary, reflection, true reflection, leads to action."[24] Unlike Mao, who clearly defines the action that self-criticism will produce, Freire never specifies any clear mode of action. To him, dialogue coincides with critical reflection, which not only is an action, but produces some sort of unspecified action. He notes that without critical reflection "action is pure activism."[25] In addition, he confuses the issue with the assertion that there exists a "true" form of critical reflection. How can people sense the existence of true critical reflection? Apparently by the action that emerges from it. How can people know that the action that emerges from it comes from true critical reflection? If the action is liberatory and revolutionary. The tautological trap.

This is where Freire runs into problems. Mao most definitely promotes an ideological transformation of society that overlays Marx's claims about historical materialism. Freire hints at these ideas, but remains vague. Regardless, in the case of Mao, the establishment of The People's Republic of China had already happened. Land was being redistributed. Collective and cooperative use of what was formerly private property was being instituted. Private property was being seized or purchased by the Party. In other words, definite aspects of economic material conditions and the capitalist mode of production had changed in China by the time Mao proposes his ideologically driven education.[26] This is not to say that Mao and other communists were not educating urban and rural peoples against imperialism and capitalism before they took power, but rather that before they took power (and after, for that matter) they included ideological education with armed resistance[27] and concrete changes in the material structure of imperialism and capitalism. This represents the most significant difference between Mao's claims about ideological education and Freire's pre-revolution aims for ideological transformation. Freire only offers the ideological dimension without considering the (armed) physical resistance and material changes required for revolution.[28] Mao's ideological education focuses on transforming the minds of the people who still carry bourgeois thoughts. He makes this clear:

> New cadres have their shortcomings. They have not been long in the revolution and lack experience, and unavoidably some have brought with them vestiges of the unwholesome ideology of the old society, remnants of the ideology of petty-bourgeois individualism. But such shortcomings can be gradually eliminated through education and tempering in the revolution.[29]

Freire vaguely hints at this idea later in the final chapter of *Pedagogy of the Oppressed*,[30] but again it is the omission of the armed struggle and the concrete changes of material conditions that preceded the ideological reeducation that leaves his comments on changing ideological perspectives hollow and, more frustratingly, able to be absorbed into soft liberal pedagogical strategies of the middle class.

Additionally, the pedagogy of North Korean revolutionary leader Kim Il-sung reinforces the differences between Mao and Freire. Again, like Mao, Che, Fidel, and Lenin (all of whom Freire quotes during the final chapter), he personally took up arms and fought against the forces of imperialism. Eventually, he oversaw education in North Korea. In his book, *On Socialist Pedagogy*, he clearly articulates, in rhetoric and language very similar to Mao, that ideological education must produce a very specific type of human. He states:

> We must make ardent revolutionaries and true Communists of all our working people, children, and youth. This means, in brief, turning them into people equipped with a revolutionary world outlook. If people acquire this outlook, they can gain a scientific understanding of nature and society, analyze and judge everything from the working-class standpoint and fight in defense of working-class interests. They will not succumb to any difficulties or trials but will be able to struggle with all devotion to overthrow the landlord and capitalist classes and the exploiter society and build socialism and communism.[31]

Kim makes this statement in 1970, over twenty years after the establishment of the Democratic People's Republic of North Korea. During the previous twenty-two years, Kim had already established massive changes in the material conditions and the mode of production in North Korea. Thus, an ideological education served to maintain "hatred for the . . . landlords and capitalists."[32] Therefore, ideological education must have three things: 1) A previous change in material conditions and the mode of production (revolutionary shifts in political-economy), all of which had occurred in the nations with the revolutionaries of whom Freire refers in the final chapter of *Pedagogy of the Oppressed*.[33] 2) Very specific language about who are the opposition, why they are the opposition, and what must be done about or to the opposition. Specificity is necessary in order to fully resist and fight against the opposition. 3) The goal must be clearly identified, e.g. Communism. Freire fails to be specific and his failure of specificity results in the easy integration of his ideas into the soft liberal pedagogical strategies of the middle class.

He does not specifically identify the antagonism of capitalism versus communism. He rarely mentions bourgeois and proletariat or owners and workers. This leaves his work in a precarious space where when he invokes the necessity for critical thinking and dialogue, nobody can be quite sure what they must think about or what they must specifically talk about. For example, instead of presenting lists of myths[34] as myths to be demythologized, in exorcist like processes of dialogue and critical reflection, Mao, Kim, and the others directly deposit oppositional myths to counter the mythology of the oppressors. Beyond this comes the attachment of the oppositional myths to material conditions, the new mode of production, and the use of force to be sure that whatever mythology retained from the oppressor is removed from the society materially, not just ideologically. Under every myth lies concrete objective conditions. Instead of addressing a myth via ideology, address the underlying concrete material conditions and take all of it out of mythology and bring it into material reality.

In *Pedagogy in Process*, Freire comes close to addressing this specific issue by comparing the conditions of Brazil and Chile during significant shifts in political and economic circumstances with the goals and practices of education during these shifts and then offering advice to the leaders in Guinea-Bissau. Ultimately, he muddles changes in material conditions with changes in ideological positions when he writes, "They need a material point of reference within the transformation that is taking place, capable of giving them visibility in the eyes of the great majority within [Guinea-Bissau]. In other words, it is necessary that the majority perceives a real need to read and write, which would not have existed if the concrete context had continued to function traditionally."[35] To stress the point, the great majority does not need to perceive anything, but rather the changes in material conditions predetermine the necessary behaviors within a concrete context. If survival in an economic structure requires people to read and write, then people will read and write without any sort of conscious realization. The goals of ideological education, as per Mao and Kim, point toward specific demands in order for Communism to prevail within the concrete context. In these cases, ideological education serves as an objective process with concrete functions and not a subjective realization of the great majority.

Furthermore, Mao asserts, "We must have faith in the masses and we must have faith in the Party."[36] Again, Freire omits the faith in the Party,[37] but keeps the faith in the masses. He proclaims, "Faith in people is an *a priori* requirement for dialogue."[38] It seems that any declaration of faith,[39] in just about any context, requires a move from objectivity and materiality to subjectivity and ideology (not to mention spirituality). Mao reiterates, "We must have faith, first, that the peasant masses are ready to advance step by step along the road of socialism under the leadership of the Party, and second, that the Party is capable of leading the peasants along this road. These two points are the essence of the matter, the main current."[40] Freire certainly articulates the necessity of this symbiotic relationship between a revolutionary leader or Party and the people in much of his early work, but rather than focus on the material conditions associated with this relationship he tends to "idealize and romanticize revolutionary leaders"[41] rather than to articulate a more materialist analysis of revolutionary situations required to transform the concrete structures of an oppressive reality.[42] For instance, according to Jim Walker, Freire regards "class divisions inherent in oppressive society as obliterated by the nationalist revolution, so that what remains in the struggle is almost entirely cultural."[43] Therefore, in all of these cases, Freire focuses on the cultural and ideological in the context of faith and virtually omits the economic and the material, whereas Mao explicitly includes both.

Faith in people and its relationship to concrete economic and material conditions appears fairly straightforward in Mao's theory and practice. Faith involves the organization and mobilization of the collective energy of the masses to participate in productive labor.[44] This means that education must not only require productive labor, but also transform the cultural practices of the people to include mass collective and cooperative labor. Revolutionary leaders must have faith in the energy and sense of duty in the people and the people must have faith in the vision of the leaders or the Party to build a new society, e.g. socialism or communism. The building of a vast economic and material infrastructure to facilitate the outpouring of the people's energy and productive labor with a new mode of production underlies the notions of mutual faith. In other words, the people need the change in material structure to develop faith in the revolutionary leadership or the Party and the revolutionary leadership or the Party must have faith that upon the building of a new economic and material structure that the people will collectively participate in productive labor or a new mode of production.

Mao describes this process when he addresses women, "With the completion of agricultural cooperation, many co-operatives are finding themselves short of labor. It has become necessary to arouse the great mass of women who did not work in the fields before to take their place on the labor front . . . China's women are a vast reserve of labor power. This reserve should be tapped in the struggle to build a great socialist country."[45] He also asserts, "In order to build a great socialist society it is of the utmost importance to arouse the broad masses of women to join in productive activity."[46] The key rhetorical phrases that illustrate the idea of faith in the people or the masses fall inside the matrix of a broad ideological vision foregrounded by dramatic shifts in the economic mode of production. Rhetoric like "arouse the great mass," "the vast reserve of labor power," and "to build a great socialist country" highlight the point where materialism meets idealism. In other words, revolutionary work involves a change in material structure with ideological training in order to produce faith in a vision of another possible world. In Mao's case, a socialist and communist world.

Freire rarely mentions socialism or communism. As he describes the shifts in Guinea-Bissau, he writes "Thus experiments were begun in 1975 which would later be extended in 1976, to integrate productive labor with the normal school activities, with the intention of combining work and study so that, as far as possible, the former might provide direction for the latter and that, together, they might form a unity."[47] He implies that the integration of labor into education provides a concrete path to expanding the production of goods required for basic survival, such as food. For example, students worked in the granaries and the gardens while attending middle school.[48] A vast workforce through education generates the proletarianization of the youth or an emergence of class consciousness among peasants who previously only worked for subsistence rather than collectively for expanded production. Faith involves the belief that peasants will share the faith-based vision to transform into the proletariat and develop its corresponding consciousness. Freire adds that this is also the case for adults. Thus, material economic based changes or the change in the mode production could inform the subsequent ideological transformation. Unfortunately, Freire's main focus remains vague and revolves around the ideological changes rather than the material changes. This is because Freire's work lacks the specific grand vision of socialism or communism (or even anti-capitalism) attached to ideological changes. Rather, he only imagines a vague notion of humanization.

Admittedly, he mentions capitalism and socialism in "Letter 11" in *Pedagogy in Process*, which highlights his obvious knowledge of Marx and the labor theory of value along with a tempered critique of capitalism. The fact that he never mentions capitalism or socialism in any of the other sixteen letters reveals his lack of commitment and perhaps his suspicion of socialism (whether of the Soviets or the Chinese or any other "socialist" nation of the time). It also reveals his failure to critique capitalism in relation to education.

Regardless, he does very briefly and vaguely mention these ideas.

Freire's Assumption of Educator Power

Finally, Freire assumes the power of educators whom he posits as subjects with power over powerless students who are objects.[49] He offers an extremely popular list that explains the educator-student relationship within the matrix of "banking education." This list must be understood in its historical context and, much like the famous list of demands of the Communist Party in Germany in Marx and Engels' *Communist Manifesto*, runs the risk of total decontextualization by both proponents and opponents.

Regardless, aside from the obvious fact that educators will have more knowledge than students because they study specific information and aim to teach it to students in fields that stray far from experiential knowledge based in daily cultural practice, the questions of teacher power that arise are: Do educators really have power over students in the ways that Freire suggests? Are not educators also objects in educational systems according to Freire? The very oppressor/oppressed binary exists in the life of educators, as well. Educators are themselves victims of domination in finely tuned hierarchies. So the assumption of educator power and the educator as subject fails to explain the situation of educators. Yet, those who promote

Freire's work still assume this educator-student relationship in this simplistic form.

In fact, Freire addresses one of the problems of his assumptions about the educator-student relationship when he writes, "As the oppressors dehumanize others and violate their rights, they themselves also become dehumanized."[50] Simply put, educators located within the hierarchal structure of capitalist educational systems comprise a dehumanized class of people who are concretely and proportionately oppressed at each descending rung of the hierarchy from the School Board to the Superintendent to College Presidents to Deans and Department Chairs all the way down to the adjunct, part-time, and substitute educators. Each oppresses and dehumanizes the next lowest on the ladder by structural default.

More significantly, and to use Freire's own logic, the hierarchy determines how the oppressor mindset internalizes in each strata as it manifests into an entire structure of dehumanization. It seems amiss that Freire wants oppressors to recognize their position as oppressors (and as oppressed), and in this case, educators as oppressors (and as oppressed), with the aim to educate students to recognize their own position as oppressed with the goal to eventually form a dialogical bond that incites resistance against other perpetrators of oppression (the dominant class). This represents an attempt to utilize Hegel's dialectic[51] that is further complicated by Freire's lack of specificity. The positional terrain of oppressor and oppressed becomes muddled and decontextualized amidst a superstructure of clearly defined material and ideological positions.

It appears clear that Freire aims to analogize the oppressor/oppressed with the bourgeois/proletariat (or capitalist/worker) as dialectical relationships, but while Marx claims that capitalists become objectified and are subject to the mode of capitalist production,[52] Freire fails to clearly articulate the analogous position of educators within the modes of educational production. He clearly explains in great detail (and in objective terms) how and why educators are oppressors of students but does not explain in great detail how and why educators are themselves oppressed. Unfortunately, he leaves the oppression of educators firmly within the realm of subjectivity and avoids the objective nature of how and why educators are themselves oppressed, i.e. educators become dehumanized because they oppress students or their oppression and dehumanization resides in their minds and so they must recognize this oppressor mindset in order to critique and, subsequently, change their minds.

Two central aspects of power arise in relation to the teachers/student binary as well as the teacher within an educational hierarchy. The first requires a look at power itself. The second requires an examination of the teacher within an educational hierarchy. Finally, all of this requires a reexamination of the banking method.

Freire's entire pedagogy depends on the validity of one idea: critical thinking. He never bothers to consider whether the masses desire to think critically. He never considers the possibility that perhaps the masses want to be told what they want. He also never envisions a society of any sort where all opportunities for the masses (or anyone else) to think critically becomes structurally impossible. Yet, pedagogues hang their scholarship on this shaky idea and lament, "If we can only get them to think critically . . ." The response to their lament from the working class may be: "Why should we bother?"

Freire stands on an unstable foundation, during a period of revolution and a period where Stalinism and Maoism manifested their totalitarian governing. In order to maintain some of the basic tenants of Maoism, in particular, Freire must promote some caveats to situate his work outside of these said totalitarian frameworks. Thus, he produces his own contradictory claims. He wants to maintain Mao, but cannot fully reconcile Mao with humanization, liberation, and freedom. Instead of riding Mao to the end by promoting a socialist banking method of education, which would guarantee, to some extent, that the masses practice socialism, he counters Mao and aims to reconcile two conflicting ideas: authoritarian rule (of the proletariat?) and critical thinking. Freire maintains a virtually untenable position with the "young" Marx and his idea of species-being and Mao's model of *leading* the masses.[53] Perhaps critical thinking may have fit into his pedagogy with greater ease had he not so loyally stuck with Mao's theory and practice. Regardless, Freire produces his own contradiction and maintains it throughout his work.

Freire refers to "the masses" frequently in his work. Teachers live as part of the masses and as official technicians for the masses. Within this framework, as both masses and official technicians for the masses, teachers secure the responsibility of both reporting to and being reported to from lower and higher rungs within hierarchal structures of power. Power circulates around bureaucracy as well as ascends and descends bureaucratically within this educational arrangement of the masses. Teachers, again, serve this dual role while students do not. Students exist solely as the masses while teachers exist professionally to maintain the hierarchy and bureaucracy in play. Freire, essentially, proposes that students develop this dual role and add to the teacher's existence within the structure of shared technicians. Students must learn and teach to ensure the maintenance of the structure while teachers operate in the same manner. Critical thinking and application should offer the vector to achieve this symbiotic relationship and its relation to whatever power happens to be presiding over the entire process.

Problems arise when power becomes unlocatable or even irrelevant in the teacher/student relationship. For instance, what if students in their role as the masses do not want to participate as teachers or technicians in maintenance of an unlocatable or irrelevant power, particularly when teachers serve as specific technicians of an uncertain power? Students both connect and disconnect when teachers describe their students to their students. This results in a withdrawal from the process altogether. Baudrillard notes that "That's what professionals are there for . . . to tell the masses what they want . . . and [the masses] assume this massive transfer of responsibility with joy, because it is simply neither obvious, nor of great interest to know, to will, to have faculties or desire. [. . .] Not only do people [the masses] surely not want to be told what they want, but they don't even want to know it, and it's not even certain that they want to want."[54] Rather than engage in a dialogical relationship with teachers, who represent some sort of abstraction of power by proxy, the masses or students as the masses allow themselves the privilege to disengage from functions of responsibilization. Power is out there somewhere and teachers have come to report what it is and how it works while students respond in a way that supports Baudrillard's description: "The masses know that they know nothing and they have no desire to know. The masses know they are powerless, and they don't want power."[55] Freire's examples in Guinea-Bissau epitomize this very notion of distal power and teachers as proximal representatives and students as the masses of objects of blank reproduction.

The mistake educators make involves the egocentric assumption that student disengagement points to signs of "stupidity and passivity," but as Baudrillard confirms, "The masses are very snobbish . . . [they] sovereignly delegate the faculty of choice to someone else, in a sort of game of irresponsibility, ironic challenge, sovereign lack of will, or secret ruse."[56] Educators in all facets of the educational structure follow in the path of the masses, since they exist within the confines of the masses. Teachers, in particular, also push away responsibilization as they simultaneously proclaim, with conviction and sincerity, their own loyal and faithful duty to their students and the institution(s) they represent. Administrators follow this same example, despite their distance from the masses. Education becomes a ruse, a game, a process of mass simulation. A simulation of which Freire did not understandably grasp within the period of revolutionary struggle. Problems arise with power when the ruse and the game become obvious, in the period well after revolutionary struggle, where critical pedagogues simulate dialogical bonds via charades of institutional power and disingenuous rejections of that same power. The power is very simply a lack of power at all levels coupled with the inability to locate the power *because* of the lack of power. This, while they pretend the power still exists and while they pretend to resist this power by avoiding the fact that it does not exist. In short, simulated power and simulated resistance to power.

All educators, whether administrators or classroom teachers, and most notably tenured pedagogues of the middle class at the highest rated institutions, paradoxically continue to practice education the way Colonial Kurtz continued to practice WW2 style barbarity in *Apocalypse Now*, despite being in the Vietnam War. In the film General Corman warns, "[Kurtz is] out there operating without any decent restraint. Totally beyond the pale of any acceptable human conduct. And he is still in the field commanding his troops."[57] Educators, still in classrooms, paradoxically operate with every bit of restraint, as if the 1960s never took place and as if revolutionary struggles never happened. But like Kurtz, they are still out there teaching. Unlike Kurtz, who offers cutthroat violence, and an absolute reign of tyrannical authority, critical pedagogues and critical educators of the liberal middle class promote and practice education as friends and cohorts with students who no longer buy any of it, but instead play the game. Kurtz attacked; educators divert. This is not because nothing good can happen in education, but rather because nothing else can happen in this framework except a shallow and hollow liberal middle-class driven preservation and perpetuation of symbolic and almost fanciful engagements with concrete material conditions through a subjective idealist displacement.

Educators on a mission to alter the system, who approach educational institutions, like Captain Richard Colby approached Colonial Kurtz,[58] must conform to the dictates of the system led by those who function through a structural inertia in order to maintain its structure (or they simply do not gain entrance). All of the mechanisms keep running and middle-class pieces are inserted to administer and teach students who already know "this is how it works" and have no interest in the process or to change the process, but instead, disinterestedly practice the necessary ways to enter it in order to keep it running. Basically, everyone pretends that power exists for the sake of simulating resistance. In all of this, no educators of the middle class want the system to actually change. There is too much to lose. (Send the middle-class kid to rural Mexico!) The teacher/student relationship functions in critical circles as a pseudo-dialogue with questions and answers playing and replaying as a game of call and response, a middle-class ruse from and for superficial masses.

In terms of power, all those within the framework of education know power, see power, and may even despise power, but this does little to nothing to inspire any serious resistance to power, especially in an anti-capitalist and pro-working-class form of resistance. Since power exists as a ghost that becomes visible in brief moments through statistics or sensational newscasts and social media posts, it never dawns on those from the liberal middle class in education that power rests within the very structure they must perpetuate. This represents the ambiguity of power that Freire juggles in his work, especially in his later writing.[59]

Moreover, this also epitomizes the type of artificial and officious power (and reactions to power) that circulates around educational hierarchies, bureaucracies, and institutions, in general. Again to refer to Baudrillard, power in education reflects a broader institutional power that exposes itself as a farcical simulation or a transparent hologram constructed to produce its own dimensions of authority *and* its own dimensions of resistance (or its own reversible pretense of potency and impotence). An all-inclusive charade where the maintenance of all its dimensions must be serviced continually in order to preserve its overall structure. In fact, this is how the illusion of critical thinking maintains in what appears as critical and what appears as thinking. Baudrillard offers the example of Patrick Le Lay of TF1, the French television channel. Le Lay states, "Let's be realistic: the job of TF1 is to help Coca-Cola sell its products. For an advertising campaign to work properly, the viewer's brains have to be accessible. The goal of our programs is to make them available, by entertaining them, relaxing them between two messages. What we sell to Coca-Cola is relaxed-brains time."[60] Education works in much the same way as TF1, although not primarily as a means to advertise a lifestyle or an ideology, but rather as a system of simulated power that exposes its own power, but also adds its own outrage or denunciation of its power (critical thinking). In education, the statement might read like this: "Let's be realistic: The job of educational institutions are to make sure that the county, state, and the federal governments maintain a budget and keep all investment in education as low as possible. For an educational institution to work properly, wages cannot be too high and labor should be precarious. The goal is to make everyone believe that we do everything we can for teachers and students. What we sell to people is the idea that educational institutions care about education." Superintendents, Administrators, Department Chairs, etc. will openly admit the power of economy over education while they and others in education (teachers, professors, and students) "critically" denounce it a moment later, yet they all adhere to every economic dictate.

Le Lay and educational technocrats share a universal exposure of the power, specifically that of the economic base. The educational technocrats differ because they expose the simulated power *and its counterpart outrage* via "critical thinking." Baudrillard adds, "Le Lay takes away the only power we had left. He steals our denunciation. *This* is the real scandal. Otherwise, how could you explain the general outrage when he revealed an open secret?"[61] The adherence and allegiance to the system of budgets in education is an open secret. The obvious advantages of the bourgeois and middle class in education is an open secret. An example comes from the structural rift and inherent competition between full-time tenured faculty (the middle class in education) and part-time adjunct faculty (the working class in education). It is an open secret that full-time tenured faculty must (and do) serve their own economic interests that conflicts with the economic interests of part-time adjunct faculty. For example, all faculty must promote their courses in order to prevent class cancelations. One particular example involves correspondence between a full-time tenured faculty member, a department chair, and an adjunct instructor relayed on an anonymous part-time faculty forum. The full-time tenured faculty member writes:

> I am requesting that you contribute once again to the promotional document that was started by our colleague last semester in order to share what we are doing in [our department] and give our students a chance to see what might interest them in future classes. If you are teaching in the spring, can you please add to or update your class info to reflect the theme or topics that you'll be teaching? Then, we can share it with our students as they are making decisions about enrolling in their classes!

In response, a part-time adjunct instructor states this:

> I know this promotional doc was made with the best intentions, but . . . there are some potential implications for adjuncts that should probably be explored. We really have no idea what enrollment will look like in the spring . . . If enrollment drops drastically next semester, a great many adjuncts can expect to be out of work. ***In light of this possibility, creating an advertisement for your course carries with it the added incentive of a market competition in which the stakes are quite high. What it might actually mean is that some of you will have health care next semester, and some of us won't.***

Next, the Department Chair added this in response to the adjunct:

Thanks,

> You make a smart, humane point, and you're right that spring is a huge question mark right now and ***everyone, particularly part-time faculty, is feeling super anxious.*** I hope you believe me when I say that I do (and will do) everything I can to make part-time faculty whole. I still think that this document/project serves a noble, though limited, purpose that could end up protecting part-time jobs in the end. ***I am repelled by the logic of competition that inevitably burrows its way into our work. In truth, though, we are always competing for students to some degree, with other schools, with other departments.***
>
> Part of the project's purpose was in fact to protect fall sections of these courses, a great many of which were taught by part-time faculty. What I can tell you is that all of our specialty courses did very well this semester due to sustained and varied promotional strategies, and in the end, that protects part-time jobs. ***Keep in mind that there is the contractual possibility that a fulltime faculty member will bump a part-time faculty member in the event of a section cancelation.*** It's gross, but it has happened. Since these specialty courses are often taught by fulltime faculty as part of their load, it is particularly important that we get them to fill.

Le Lay shows open contempt and cynicism to people while he reveals the open secret of the economic base and structural obscenities of the capitalist mode of production and market system. The Department Chair, like Le Lay, reveals the open secret of the economic base and the structural obscenity of the educational market system, but unlike Le Lay, the Department Chair simultaneously, paradoxically, and ironically (and unashamedly) denounces the very same system. The Department Chair shows the universal disingenuousness and impotence within the structure by both upholding and denouncing it with officious allegiance and sympathetic outrage. Thereby, delegitimizing and superficializing the denunciation and, thus, eliminating it. Yes, power is an open secret in education.

To be more specific, the first instructor, clueless to any sort of economic dimension (as are many tenured professors of the middle class) presents an inherently competitive advertising campaign for courses. The adjunct instructor presents an argument that exposes the market system within the educational structure and even cites the possibility of losing health insurance as a concrete and objective deficiency in the educational market structure. Finally, the Department Chair follows Le Lay when they confess the deficiencies of the market system while demonstrating allegiance to the market system. The liberal Department Chair inserts the additional pseudo-moral dimension when they also denounce the system. In essence, the Department Chair's email could have simply read: "I feel really bad about it, but the system is competitive. I love you. Now, deal with it!" Herein lies the crux of the liberal position of the middle class in educational structures: in terms of power, it is a position that both serves power and resists power in a simulated all-inclusive process. Baudrillard succinctly describes it: "Only those who show no concern for contradiction or critical consideration in their acts and discourse, by this very means, shed full light, without remorse or ambiguity, on the absurd and extravagant character of the state of things, through the play of objective irony."[62]

To return to Freire, this economic base and its accompanying simulation foregrounds the teacher/student relationship. Forces of power, whether understood in simulation or not, shape the position of teachers and students. The market structure and the capitalist mode of production offers teachers prospects like "Right to Work" contracts from Charter Schools where teachers can be dismissed at any time for any reason without any recourse. Part-time adjunct employment where schools offer per course contracts without any reasonable assurance of employment, i.e. ***there is the contractual possibility that a full-time faculty member will bump a part-time faculty member in the event of a section cancelation.*** Semester to semester or year to year contracts without benefits at the K-12 level. More and more part-time K-12 teachers teach two courses at one school and then drive to another school across town to teach more courses. These factors greatly undermine the power of the teacher in a classroom and render Freire's notion of the teacher with power and the student without power obsolete.

Perhaps power *should* manifest objectively rather than in the simulation of relative power. Perhaps it *should* primarily attack the market system, the capitalist economic base, and the capitalist mode of production. Freire focuses on what he calls the "banking concept," which "turns [students] into . . . receptacles to be filled by the teacher."[63] Perhaps a more radical form of the banking concept will serve to transform, liberate, and revolutionize the masses and eliminate the aforementioned contradictions. Had Freire followed Mao and the like more closely, education may have revolutionized into radical banking where students receive anti-capitalist training both materially and ideologically.

Freire's famous list is as follows:

> This solution is not (nor can it be) found in the banking concept. On the contrary, banking education maintains and even stimulates the contradiction through the following attitudes and practices, which mirror oppressive society as a whole:
>
> (a) the teacher teaches and the students are taught;
> (b) the teacher knows everything and the students know nothing;
> (c) the teacher thinks and the students are thought about;
> (d) the teacher talks and the students listen—meekly;
> (e) the teacher disciplines and the students are disciplined;
> (f) the teacher chooses and enforces his choice, and the students comply;
> (g) the teacher acts and the students have the illusion of acting through the action of the teacher;
> (h) the teacher chooses the program content, and the students (who were not consulted) adapt to it;
> (i) the teacher confuses the authority of knowledge with his or her own professional authority, which she

> and he sets in opposition to the freedom of the students;
> (j) the teacher is the Subject of the learning process, while the pupils are mere objects.
>
> It is not surprising that the banking concept of education regards men as adaptable, manageable beings.[64]

To repeat, perhaps transformation, liberation, and revolution arrive through radical banking, (a form of education that can or must continue well after liberation and revolution, as well). The above list certainly correlates with many of the commands found in educational practice through things like standardized testing or state and federal standards like the Common Core, but all of these standards produce and reinforce neoliberal capitalist power. Teachers may actually "know everything" while the students "know nothing" because teacher training involves learning the practice of standardization, particularly in testing. Teachers have the answers to the test. Objectively, students must do well on these tests. Therefore, teachers must be depositors of information into student banks. Of course, to state that this makes teachers subjects and students objects appears absurd, since the teacher serves as as much of an object as the student in the broader simulation of power through the standardized inertia that perpetuates capitalism. Incidentally, this banking concept does in fact produce a population of loyal, dedicated, subservient, and docile people who almost unquestioningly reproduce the daily activities across the matrix of capitalism.

When Freire subjectifies teachers and objectifies students, he decontextualizes both from actual institutions of power, such as the capitalist mode of production and the state. He microscopically views the classroom as an insular space where students ironically "read the world."[65] Teachers serve merely as managers of the capitalist state whose power always remains subject to the dictates of the capitalist state. David Smail advances a clear description of this power. He proposes:

> Power is generated within and through social institutions. The institutions of power operate independently of particular individuals and at varying distances from them, affecting them via almost unimaginably complex lines of influence that travel through individuals as well as through other institutions. The further away from the individual person a particular social institution is, the more powerful it is likely to be and the more individuals it will affect. Apparently paradoxically, the nearer to the (average) individual an institution is, the less its total power is likely to be, though, owing to the distortion of his or her perspective, it will be experienced by that individual as more powerful.[66]

Since institutions of power operate independently of any particular individual, the individual teacher only serves the institution and does not carry any actual power. More accurately, the teacher lives at the mercy of the distal power that capitalism manifests. The teacher operates as a simple medium of information, rather than as an independent subject with independent power. Distal economic and governmental powers prescribe the actions of the teacher. This distance creates an all-inclusive rationale for every single decision within the hierarchal structure of education. To ask why only generates futile responses, regardless of the disingenuous morality many educators attach. Disciplinary actions? Policy. Low Wages? Policy. Right to Work? Policy. Standardized Tests? Policy. Frequent Observations? Policy. Budget? Policy. Strike? Policy. No Contract? Policy. Freire appears to subjectify teachers because of the proximity of the teacher to the student. The teacher appears to be an individual of power to the student.

For instance, the Department Chair lives as a vector of distal institutional power who appears as an individual with power, but merely follows policies generated at some other level of power, thus, relieving them of any personal responsibility in the matter of scheduling, i.e. you may be displaced, but that's the policy. These "complex lines of influence" allow for an institutional impotency, one that Department Chairs and others in education need. Without this officious impotence, face to face contact with those lower on the hierarchy might be unbearable (power from the top to the bottom, but nobody with any real power. No subjects. Only objects. No power. Only a simulation of power). Smail's "complex lines of influence" allow for Baudrillard's simulation of power, or a vast system of farcical play. In fact, the entire "critical pedagogy" movement (and its industrially produced curriculums and materials) exists to circulate impotence in order to make bearable the concrete objective conditions of both the hierarchy within educational institutions and the class structure which informs them. Liberal pedagogues of the middle class cannot exist without this complex system that excuses their obligatory allegiance to capitalism.

The teacher does not think, and the students cannot be thought about. The teacher does not act, and the students do not have the illusion of acting through the inaction of the teacher. The teacher does not choose the program content, and the students (who are consulted) do not adapt to it. The teacher does not confuse the authority of knowledge with his or her own professional authority, and they do not set it in opposition to the lack of freedom of the students. Finally, the teacher is not the Subject of the learning process while the pupils are mere objects. Both are objects.

Teachers as objects receive their appearance of subjectivity or power from their institutional backing. They serve as representatives of power, but the power that they represent simply signifies an appearance of power. This does not mean that the appearance of power negates the effects of power, but it does not produce the kind of subjectivity that Freire claims to exist.

Perhaps this predicament can be understood by examining a radical form of the banking concept that illustrates not only an acknowledgement of teachers and students as objects, but also in the production of objects as revolutionary objects who appear as representatives of clear institutional power. Rather than play a game of critical thinking, in which a farcical call and response ruse that disingenuously appears as critical thinking, teachers may be able to allow or inform the implosion of one objectified power toward the emergence of another type of objectified power. Without the prospect for subjectivity, the revolutionary object may emerge.

Had Freire followed Mao all the way, perhaps he would have come to this conclusion. Mao's vision of freedom firmly hinged upon a collective subjectivity which relied upon the masses of objectified individuals. In addition to Mao, Kim's ideologically opposite "socialist pedagogy" can be referenced to fully understand Freire's inaccuracies and to grasp how the discourse of capital through its middle class dominate educational settings. Again to refer to his text *On Socialist Pedagogy*, the concrete reality of objectification materializes without contradiction and without illusions of individual subjective freedom through something like critical thinking. Kim's revolutionary pedagogy produces a radical banking concept for revolution where humans operate as revolutionary objects. Kim's pedagogy involves the shocking displacement of subjective freedom, but this is already the predicament in capitalist education with its simulation of subjects where power becomes unlocatable, disguised, and simulated. In radical banking or revolution, subjects, objects, and power are clear.

At the very base of Freire's critical pedagogy and his politics resides the basic binaries that present the world as split into colonializer/colonized, oppressor/oppressed, subject/object. This means that his masses are objects in relation to very few subjects. A more astute understanding of the predicament in capitalist education as well as in capitalist society highlights that every human is an object in a capitalist system, even capitalists, because the mode of production dictates this condition. Marx states in *Capital Volume 1*, "It is evident that this does not depend on the will, either good or bad, of the individual capitalist. Under free competition, immanent laws of capitalist production confront the individual capitalist as a coercive force external to him."[67] Therefore, objectivity, whether from the capitalist mode of production or not, is the most basic tenet embedded within widespread (or global) productive activity, from which an educational structure emerges.

Kim suggests that education must "turn [the masses] into people equipped with a revolutionary outlook [and they must] . . . analyze and judge everything from the working-class standpoint and fight in defense of working-class interests."[68] He continues, "It is not an easy matter to establish a revolutionary world outlook. People cannot shape such an outlook in a few days by one or two preaching sessions. It is formed, developed and consolidated through some stages of ideological development by tireless ideological education and practical struggle."[69] Kim's goals for revolutionary education are overt and clear rather than disguised or misrepresented as critical thinking. In this case, a continuous anti-capitalist education requires *students to be receptacles* (objects) that must, without any choice nor critical thinking, internalize the working-class viewpoint in order to "develop hatred for the landlord and capitalist classes and for capitalism and imperialism."[70] This is not to suggest that Mao's or Kim's ideas for education should be instituted, but rather to highlight how capitalist education serves the same goals as "socialist" education, which is to create the capitalist object. The main distinction is that in educational institutions that utilize Freire's pedagogy, liberals of the middle class mystify the operation of power and the subject/object relationship.

Imagine what a working-class education may look like through Kim's extreme language. This puts capitalist education from the middle class into perspective. Education for the working class simply does not exist within capitalist educational institutions. The attempt to insert middle and upper middle-class teachers and students into working class, working poor, or impoverished international spaces does not develop the viewpoint of the "working class." Students do not return from rural Mexico with hatred for capitalism, rather they represent figures of class advantage who work as representatives for the capitalist class. Just try to imagine the opposite occurring among classes. Imagine working-class folks sent to help the middle class escape from their suburban homes and their security. In fact, in some cases, this served as the primary goal in both Mao and Kim's educational systems.

Kim's "practical struggle" involved active, overt, and objective anti-capitalist practice. Just as every aspect of education within a capitalist structure reproduces capitalism, every aspect of education in an anti-capitalist structure should reproduce anti-capitalism.

This relates to a basic lack of awareness of the economic context that informs educational and societal practice. Educators and students of the middle class remain unaware of the economic exploitation produced by the capitalist mode of production because they exist as fully embedded in the most secure sectors of it. Entrance into impoverished and insecure spaces yields only an awareness that is represented in a song like "Do They Know It's Christmas?" which was written and performed to help the tragic mass starvation in Africa in the 1980s. Jaap Kooijman notes, "'Do They Know It's Christmas?' makes a strong distinction between 'us' celebrating Christmas in 'our world of plenty,' while 'they' in 'a world outside your window' are starving, suggesting that 'we' should be grateful that the African tragedy is happening to 'them' rather than to 'us.' As a result, the lyrics seem to invite a cynical interpretation, particularly when

U2's Bono cries out 'well tonight, thank God it's them instead of you.'"[71] Educators and prospective educators of the middle class can do nothing but interpret the condition of the working class, working poor, insecure, and impoverished populations with the same sentiment of "Thank God it's them and not me." This is because all the liberal middle class have to offer the working class is a vague hope of entering the middle class. Nothing revolutionary or liberatory. Only a: "perhaps you can be included, too." This is what separates capitalist education mandated and executed by the middle class compared to an education that can be described as working class.

These advantages of the middle class in educational contexts work with Freire's assertions about power within the classroom because Freire does not advocate for the working class. Rather than displace the middle class from positions of advantage, Freire aims to keep them in their places and to liberalize their minds for a slow and soft reform. Liberal niceties like inclusion or equity keep capitalism and its technicians of the middle class in place. These practices merely reinforce the banking practices that foreground capitalism. In reality, including a few working-class folks (or a few Black folks) here and there does not objectively change anything and, in fact, produces the opposite effect by reinforcing a rewards system or a lottery for the working class.

Only an entire displacement of the middle class from education will yield an education of and for the working class. Inclusion, at best, brings a few who offer working-class viewpoints, but, at worst, not only creates an appearance of economic change, but also turns working-class folks into middle-class technicians. Inclusion simply means to make a few more people middle class, but in reality, this objectively encapsulates the entire scope of education anyway! Again, imagine the opposite, working-class folks actively seeking out middle-class spaces to essentially assess, train, and then offer them the hope of someday entering the working class.

Capitalist banking concepts already exist and work in education. Therefore, by analogy, an opposite material and ideological banking approach comprises (perhaps) a path for the working class to initiate revolutionary education. The precedents set in socialist spaces present radical and revolutionary banking concepts both pre- and post- revolution.

Capitalist education and socialist education differ because capitalist education aims to continue the relative lack of exploitation and oppression of the middle class through the concrete exploitation of the working class while socialist education aims to eliminate exploitation and oppression in the entire society by teaching students about capitalist exploitation and oppression. Kim continues, "By giving education . . . to school children and students about the cruel oppression and exploitation of the peasants and workers by the landlords and capitalists in the past, they should be given a clear idea of the true colors of the landlord and capitalist classes as exploiters and the reactionary nature of capitalism."[72] Freire's opportunity to fully articulate a real pedagogy of the oppressed failed because he chose to frame oppression inside the idealist concept of humanization rather than the materialist concept of changing the mode of production, which made humanization the goal to overcome oppression instead of overcoming capitalism.

The difference between how capitalist education and socialist education manifests in society is epitomized by a comment made by a full-time tenured professor at a faculty meeting, after the cancelation of several courses to be taught by part-time instructors. The full-time tenured professor stated, "I feel so bad for the adjuncts because I can sit here at my beautiful home next to my swimming pool while they are unsure of whether they will have work and make money to take care of their families."[73] Capitalist education and its technicians of the middle class do not question property ownership. They do not question the existence of landlords. They cannot detect their own contribution to exploitation. It does not matter that they may feel bad about it. Educators like the full-time tenured professor cannot generate hatred for the capitalist mode of production because they benefit from it.

Perhaps if Freire had proposed a radical banking concept for revolution it could have resulted in the elimination of the soft liberalism that reinforces and reproduces the capitalist mode of production and its middle-class technicians. It might have plainly, unequivocally, and exclusively included educators and students of the working class in order to unambiguously develop "hatred" for capitalism. Just as educators of the middle class make their students into capitalists, "unless the teachers are Communists themselves, they will not be able to make their pupils into Communists."[74] In short, this is why Freire's pedagogy cannot be liberatory nor revolutionary and also explains why the liberal educators of the middle class promote his pedagogy. Educators of the middle class cannot be revolutionaries or liberators. Educators of the middle class do not have to proclaim that education must "turn [the masses] into people equipped with a middle-class capitalist outlook [and they must] . . . analyze and judge everything from the middle-class standpoint and fight in defense of middle-class interests" because the capitalist mode of production produces the educational structure that already does this right now.[75]

---

[1] In his article, "Neoliberalism and Postmodernity: Reflections on Freire's Later Work," Peter Roberts states, "In the early 1970s, he [Freire] endured attacks from doctrinaire Marxists and Maoists for advocating dialogical principles of political organization over mechanistic models of revolutionary change. Regarded as a naive idealist by those who believed the class struggle had its own logic independent of human interaction and intervention . . . [.]" This section may read like another retread of the arguments against Freire from the 1970s. Regardless, the overall thesis in this section explores the relationship between Freire's emphasis on individual subjectivity, use of vague rhetoric, and assumptions about the power of educators found in *Pedagogy of the Oppressed* (and other

works) and the ease of which his ideas can be and have been integrated into democratic reformist liberal pedagogy that seamlessly fit into ideology closely associated with capitalism and Neoliberism. Freire's individualism, his lack of definitive proclamations against capitalism, and his skewed concepts of power results, decades later, in the inclusion of his work into pedagogies implicitly and sometimes explicitly in support of capitalism and Neoliberalism.

[2] For a concise and somewhat comprehensive review of various critiques of Freire, please refer to the webpage below, which lists many texts under the heading of "Critical Views of Paulo Freire's Work." Blanca Facundo offers a particularly interesting critique entitled, *Freire-inspired Programs in the United States and Puerto Rico: A Critical Evaluation*.

See https://www.bmartin.cc/dissent/documents/Facundo/Ohliger1.html, from "Critical views of Paulo Freire's Work," by John Ohliger, 1995.

[3]https://www.bmartin.cc/dissent/documents/Facundo/section8.html

[4] Jean Baudrillard, *America*, 29.

[5] Or the theories of Franz Fanon.

[6] Paulo Freire, *Pedagogy of the Oppressed*, 90.

[7] Jim Walker, "The End of Dialogue: Paulo Freire on Politics and Education" from the book *Literacy and Revolution: the Pedagogy of Paulo Freire,* 131.

[8]https://www.theregister.com/Print/2007/11/20/adam_curtis_interview/

[9] Freire, *Pedagogy in Process*, 104.

[10] Ibid., 18.

[11] Diana Coben, "Paulo Freire's Legacy for Adults Learning Mathematics."

[12] Cristina Alfaro, "Developing Ideological Clarity: One Teacher's Journey" *Counterpoints* Vol. 319, p. 231-249.

[13] https://www.youtube.com/watch?v=5jTUebm73lY, John Berger, *Ways of Seeing*, Episode 4.

[14] Cristina Alfaro, "Developing Ideological Clarity: One Teacher's Journey" *Counterpoints* Vol. 319, p. 231-249.
[15] "Holiday in Cambodia," Dead Kennedys, https://genius.com/Dead-kennedys-holiday-in-cambodia-lyrics
[16] https://theoccupiedtimes.org/?p=12841, Mark Fisher, "Good for Nothing," Mar. 19, 2014.
[17] Freire, *Oppressed*, 136-137.
[18] Mao Tse-Tung, "On Protracted War," *Selected Works Volume 2*, 153-153.
[19] Freire, *Oppressed*, 55.
[20] Freire, *Oppressed*, 167.
[21] The English version is also titled as *Quotations from Chairman Mao Tse-Tung*.
[22] Mao, *Little Red Book*, 1.
[23] Ibid., 1.
[24] Freire, *Oppressed*, 66.
[25] Ibid., 66.
[26] See the book *Ideology and Practice: The Evolution of Chinese Communism* by James Chieh Hsiung, particularly the chapter entitled "The Structure of the Chinese Communist Ideology" where Hsiung explains the origins of Mao's thought in relation to Hegel and Marx as well as the necessary addition of ideological education after material conditions had been changed or after the establishment of The People's Republic of China. Several years after the publication of *Pedagogy of the Oppressed*, Freire did receive the opportunity to put his pedagogy into practice in the country of Guinea-Bissau after its liberation from Portugal.
[27] Incidentally, in his book *Pedagogy in Process, The Letters to Guinea-Bissau*, Freire implies his support for armed revolution when he quotes revolutionary Amílcar Cabral and others discussing their use of arms in the struggle for liberation. One example repeats Mao's concept of "progressive war" when a "young educator" in a "soft and gentle voice" says, "Evil persons like that, when they are caught, are punished in accord of with the people's judgement" (31). Of course, the people's judgement included execution. This is evidenced by the execution of about "one hundred people" who

were deemed responsible for the assassination of Cabral. For a more detailed look at Freire's ideas on violence see Robert Mackie's article, "Contributions to the Thought of Paulo Freire" from the book *Literacy and Revolution: the Pedagogy of Paulo Freire*.

[28] In the book *Che Guevara, Paulo Freire and the Pedagogy of Revolution*, Peter McLaren explains that "Freire was a great admirer of Amílcar Cabral, a revolutionary leader who helped to liberate Guinea-Bissau from Portuguese domination in the 1960s. Whereas Franz Fanon had urged armed intervention in Guinea-Bissau, Cabral had understood that the political education of the peasantry had to be achieved first or else the revolution would be short-lived" (146). This makes perfect sense, but Freire virtually ignores the armed violence required for revolution and the overthrow of capitalism while the revolutionaries he quotes recognized the necessity for armed revolt and also participated in armed revolt. Also, this represents a suspect understanding of Cabral's attitude toward armed revolution, since Cabral literally led an armed revolution. He was certainly careful about how and when, but he was most definitely in favor of armed revolt (See *Pedagogy in Process* 18-20). On top of this is the objective fact that the peasantry did not receive a revolutionary education before the liberation of Guinea-Bissau. This is why Freire was called upon to set up the educational system in the country after its liberation.

[29] Mao, *Little Red Book*, 22.

[30] Freire, *Oppressed*, 160-167.

[31] Kim Il-sung, *On Socialist Pedagogy*, 177-178.

[32] Ibid., 179.

[33] The only exception is Lenin, who penned *What is to be Done?* before the revolution. But again, Lenin proposes clear and explicit revolutionary changes to the material structure of society and not simply vague expressions of ideological changes.

[34] Freire, *Oppressed*, 139.

[35] Freire, *Pedagogy in Process*, 101.

[36] Mao, *Little Red Book*, 2.

[37] It is important to note that Freire fails to make a real commitment to the politics or the necessity of a revolutionary Party. He implies a

sort of alignment to the revolutionary Party in Guinea-Bissau through his comments found in the book *Pedagogy in Process*, but does not make an unconditional commitment to the use of a Party. He also implies support for Castro's Party in Cuba, but again, he generally remains noncommittal to the necessity of a Party, vanguard or otherwise.

[38] Freire, *Oppressed*, 90.

[39] An extremely interesting read is a text called "Draft of a Communist Confession of Faith" by Engels. Despite the word "faith" and the religious language and catechism organization of the text, it is firmly written from a historical materialist perspective.

[40] Mao, *Little Red Book*, 12.

[41] Mackie, "Thought of Freire," 112.

[42] Ibid., 112.

[43] Walker, "The End of Dialogue" from the book *Literacy and Revolution,* 131.

[44] The term "productive labor" is used as a general phrase. Marx describes "productive labor" and its differences from other types of labor in *Capital Volume 2* (and other texts), and Mandel spends much time on the concept of productive labor in the introduction of *Volume 2*. Mao uses the term "productive activity" and "productive forces" in several texts, and Freire uses the term "productive work," "productive activities," and "productive labor" throughout *Pedagogy in Process*. Mao and Freire use the terms interchangeably and more vaguely as any work that is productive, regardless of the economic structure, whereas Marx uses the term with a very specific definition within capitalism. It is also important to note that these are all English translations of terms. Again, the use of the term here follows Mao and Freire's more casual and all-encompassing use of the term in its English translation. See also "Productive and Unproductive Labor and Marx's Theory of Class" by Peter Meiksins, October 1, 1981 in *Review of Radical Economics*.

[45] Mao, *Little Red Book*, Section 31.

[46] Ibid., Section 31.

[47] Freire, *Pedagogy in Process*, 21.

[48] Ibid., 22.

[49] Freire, *Oppressed*, 71.

[50] Ibid., 56.
[51] Freire, *Oppressed*, 72.
[52] Marx states in *Capital Volume 1*, "It is evident that this does not depend on the will, either good or bad, of the individual capitalist. Under free competition, immanent laws of capitalist production confront the individual capitalist as a coercive force external to him" (381).
[53] See Erich Fromm's *Marx's Concept of Man*. Also see the article, "On the Origin of Species-Being: Marx Redefined" by James M. Czank who argues "that the Russian communists appropriated Marx's theory in an attempt to convince the world that their practices and theories followed his ideas" (322). No doubt Freire read Fromm's work, but unlike Fromm, who was highly critical of Soviet and Chinese communism, Freire tries to assimilate "young" Marx with Mao. Kieran Durkin notes, "Fromm sought to restore Marxism to its original form as 'a new humanism,' cleansed of the distortions of Soviet and Chinese communism." (https://www.jacobinmag.com/2020/08/erich-fromm-frankfurt-school-marxism-weimar-germany). Freire tries to follow Fromm, but his continual references and glorifying of Mao and other authoritarian leaders produces a break from Fromm.
[54] Jean Baudrillard, *Fatal Strategies*, 126-127.
[55] Ibid., 127.
[56] Ibid., 127.
[57] https://sfy.ru/transcript/apocalypse_now_ts
[58] A Captain who is given the same mission as Captain Willard in *Apocalypse Now* and ends up joining Kurtz's forces.
[59] See *Teachers As Cultural Workers: Letters to Those Who Dare Teach* by Paulo Freire, which more than any other work highlights this simulation of the teacher/student relationship amidst both the absence of and the perpetuation of power.
[60] Jean Baudrillard, *The Agony of Power*, 37-38.
[61] Ibid., 38-39.
[62] Ibid., 40.
[63] Freire, *Oppressed*, 72.
[64] Ibid., 73.
[65] Freire, *Oppressed*, 26.

[66] David Smail, *Power, Responsibility, and Freedom*, 10.
[67] Marx, *Capital Vol 1*, 381.
[68] Kim, *Socialist Pedagogy*, 177-178.
[69] Ibid., 178.
[70] Ibid., 180.
[71] Jaap Kooijman, *Fabricating the Absolute Fake: America in Contemporary Pop Culture*, 25.
[72] Ibid., 187-188.
[73] Quote taken from an actual faculty meeting via Zoom.
[74] Kim, *Socialist Pedagogy*, 223.
[75] Again, this is not suggest that the pedagogies of Mao or Kim should be instituted, but rather to highlight the entire impossibility of Freire's pedagogy as liberatory or revolutionary and also why the liberal middle class so heartily endorse it.

Chapter 6: Disconnects & Hypocrisies: Liberal Administrators and Full-Time Faculty Fight for Social Justice and Fight against Economic Justice

The structure of education centers on bureaucratic and hierarchal arrangements that include, embrace, and reward people of the middle class. People of the working class sometimes ascend to the middle class within the educational structure, but generally, like in other industries, people of the middle class dominate the structure and, therefore, perpetuate its dominance by excluding those of the working class. The bureaucracy and hierarchy includes specifically defined positions like school Presidents, Superintendents, Deans, Principals, Department Chairs, Tenured Faculty, union Faculty, Student Teachers, Aides, Students, and so on.

People of the middle class hold the great majority of positions in the upper segments of the bureaucratic and hierarchal arrangement. They are mediocre by definition. The material conditions of work within education produce these people en masse. The fact of being of the middle class produces *and generationally reproduces* mediocrity (subservience, passivity, superficiality, ignorance, etc.), which serves as an almost unconscious prerequisite to ascend up the educational ladder of security. In short, educators of the middle class must see themselves in their peers. Therefore, mediocrity informs their inherent inclusion, inevitable insertion, and repetitive practice within the educational structure, which directly serves their class interests.

With this precondition, hierarchy plays a fundamental *and* detrimental role. Entrance into ascending rungs can be intricate for educators as several factors determine entrance, all of which are determined by the very structure they reinforce. With each movement upwards comes slightly more power and security. Although slight, the difference between rungs determine levels of security, salary, benefits, retirement, and so forth. Each ascending rung structurally and materially requires specific behaviors, attitudes, and actions (sometimes by law) which reinforce the broader structure of the institution and the society. The society and culture on the outside of the educational institution determines the practices within the educational institution and favors people of the middle class, and those who work within educational institutions replicate and reproduce specific societal mores on the outside of the educational institution, thereby making the educational institution simply part of the broader societal structure. Keep in mind that this is structural; it is material; it is not moral; it is not ideological. This point must be stressed to avoid any confusion that individuals should be blamed for being passive, just smart enough, or mediocre. Rather, the middle class are mediocre and subservient because they are of the middle class and because they are of the middle class they are mediocre and subservient.

It is no secret that the structure that surrounds and envelopes educational institutions is capitalist. So educational institutions are capitalist institutions, structurally and materially, regardless of being labeled as "public" and regardless of the various persuasions (political, etc.) of the people who are positioned within the institutions. They are products (object models) of capitalism, and they reinforce capitalist modes and relations of production. Their hierarchal structure, with stringent regulations, rules, power dynamics, privileges, etc. enable them to do nothing but be products (object models) who reinforce capitalistic modes and relations of production.

For example, the vast objective differences between the full-time tenured professor and the part-time adjunct instructor epitomizes one specific place in the bureaucratic and hierarchal structure of education that magnifies this situation. This is not to say that all tenured professors come from the middle class and that all adjunct instructors come from the working class because even to get enough education to qualify as an instructor presupposes the likelihood of a middle-class background (although it should be noted that highly rated universities populated by and graduating middle [and capitalist class] students produce those who are most likely to receive full-time tenured faculty positions, which obviously informs iniquitous class representation in the concrete numbers of faculty), but rather that those who are tenured professors produce and reproduce the role that the middle class play within the broader capitalist society and the adjunct instructor produces and reproduces the role of the working class within the broader capitalist society. The material conditions of each determine these roles and inherently produce a class divide inside educational institutions.

This is also not to say that these roles are played consciously. A middle-class tenured professor does not consciously or purposely oppress adjunct instructors, at least not entirely, but rather that class positioning determines the middle-class tenured professor's treatment of adjunct instructors. It is clearly beneficial for the smooth functioning of the system to privilege the tenured faculty of the middle class because these positions allow for a general ignorance of economic and, subsequent, psychological predicaments of the working class. By analogy one can look to Noam Chomsky's media filtering to see how this works in education. He states:

> The elite domination of the media and marginalization of dissidents that results from the operation of these filters occurs so naturally that media news people, frequently operating with complete integrity and goodwill, are able to convince themselves that they choose and interpret the news "objectively" and on the basis of professional news values[.] . . . [And] given the imperatives of corporate organization and the workings of the various filters, conformity to the needs and interests of privileged sectors is essential to success. In the media, as in other major institutions,

> those who do not display the requisite values and perspectives will be regarded as "irresponsible," "ideological," or otherwise aberrant, and will tend to fall by the wayside. While there may be a small number of exceptions, the pattern is pervasive, and expected [.] . . . The media are indeed free for those who adopt the principles required for their societal purpose.[1]

Full-time tenured professors believe in their ingenuousness because the filtering process occurs well before the job offer since the "requisite values" are deeply engrained from birth into the middle class. They firmly believe that their class and hierarchal positions do not inherently produce and reproduce insecurity and oppression in the educational setting. They do not feel responsible for the precarious circumstances of the adjunct instructors of the working class and naturally fail to perceive their own perpetuation of classism. Like journalists working for *The New York Times*, they feel they have earned their positions through higher education at highly rated universities and through work and research experience in the field without realizing that their option to attend highly rated universities and their option to gain work and research experience in the field was already determined by their class position. They, without even a hint of irony, enforce bureaucratic regulations that maintain the hierarchy as acts of honesty, integrity, and duty while proclaiming allegiance to and solidarity in the values of what they call "equality" and "equity." To parallel Chomsky's claims, those who ascend to the rank of tenured track professor have already been filtered through the previous determinates or "requisite values" such as education, work, and research experience, all of which are determined by class positioning from birth. Just as there are none or very few journalists from the working class at *The New York Times*, there are none or very few tenured professors from working class at any given college or university.

By contrast, those born into the working class do not naturally develop the "requisite values" and materially or concretely do not have the option to attend highly rated universities nor gain valuable work and research experience. The values of the working class simply do not reinforce the societal purpose of education embedded in the capitalist mode of production. In contrast, educators of the working class must consciously train themselves to think like educators of the middle class and even to look and act like educators of the middle class. As Chomsky notes, "there may be a small number of exceptions," but those exceptions from the working class in the bureaucratic and hierarchal structure of education serve as token characters to the extent they copy the mediocre, subservient, and technocratic behavior and practices of the middle class and avoid behaving and practicing as those from the working class. Essentially, the bureaucratic and hierarchal structure of education operates with the same nepotism, cronyism, and tokenism as general guidelines for capitalist reproduction just as in media and just as in any other capitalist industry. People of the middle class in education will perpetuate, both consciously and unconsciously,[2] the capitalist values that reproduce the system through nepotistic, cronyistic, and tokenistic practices.

Class reproduces generationally. This is a very basic point. There exist differences between folks of the working class who first enter the middle class, either economically or spatially or both, than people of the middle class who remain in the middle class and enter middle class spaces. First generation people of the middle class from working-class backgrounds behave and think differently than people who have been in the middle class for a couple of generations. Parents of the working class who raise children in spaces inhabited by those of the middle class can easily recognize the class distinctions between them and their children. Certain ideas about the world simply do not emerge in the middle-class children that emerged in the working-class parents.

In education, folks of the working class who become educators, as Mark Fisher states, "lack the calm confidence of one born to the role."[3] Educators from the working class easily recognize the calm confidence of educators of the middle class who appear "born into the role." They appear born into the role *because they are born into the role.* For educators of the middle class, a job in education simply exists as part of the general chronological progress in life. The overwhelming anxieties that permeate educators from the working class, where to secure or lose employment, means to secure or lose life simply does not exist for educators of the middle class. To get a job is not part of the general chronological progress in life for folks of the working class, who can never be confident of getting or keeping a job, regardless of educational achievement and hard work.

One example that highlights this difference goes as follows: A full-time tenured faculty member corresponds with full-time and part-time faculty about the potential to teach college courses at an expensive local private high school. In context, according to the anonymous post, several part-time instructors were not offered courses because of budget cuts and low enrollment. The paraphrased message states:

> Blank High School wants to add college courses to their schedule next academic year through a dual-enrollment partnership with our college. It looks like the administration is already game, but we do have the opportunity to weigh in. My primary concern is whether instructors will have full academic freedom over course content and delivery.

The full-time tenured faculty member makes the differences between the perspective of the middle class and the perspective from the working class evident by noting that the main concern is "academic freedom." Again, this is in the context where many part-time instructors lost their jobs. Simply put, academic freedom is the last concern for those of the working class who need to work. Economic imperatives foreclose notions like academic freedom or most other ethical or moral considerations.

By analogy, to refer to a previous example: Latinos make up the majority (51-52%) of Border Patrol agents and one-fourth of ICE agents. The reason is evident, as Brittney Meija reports about Imperial County, California, "[Border Patrol] is a job in a county with the second-highest unemployment rate statewide at 17%. The Border Patrol is one of the top employers in Imperial County."[4] People need to work. Latinos who work as Border Patrol and ICE agents cannot stop to ponder the ethical or moral aspects of policing other Latinos because the economic base determines morals and ethics or lack thereof. This exemplifies predicaments that folks of the working class face, and that people of the middle class do not face. Perhaps people of the middle class can ponder ethics and morality because of their objective security, but folks of the working class cannot. Here the full-time faculty member illustrates a class-based perspective and clearly does not conceive of nor comprehend the realities of the working class.

Another example that epitomizes the inherent structural conflicts evident in class division: One labor union representative messaged the college faculty about solidarity with others who planned a rent strike. While part-time faculty mainly voiced their support, several full-time tenured faculty members aggressively responded against the rent strike. As reported, one particular message implicitly summarizes the structural antagonism between classes from a middle-class conservative perspective:

> What will the property owners, who use the rent money received from tenants to pay their bills, do when that income is stopped? This "movement" causes a larger ripple effect and is encouraging people to be dishonest and fail to fulfill the promise they made when they signed their lease or loan paperwork. America is a Free Enterprise system where hard work determines success. Housing is not a "right," it is a privilege based on the amount of effort exerted to earn to pay for it. The more work, the more money you earn equals a nicer place you can live. Just because some people want the government to pay for their housing does not add a "right" to the Constitution. There are already eviction moratoriums being put into place to protect people. This Rent Strike will also create an outcome of negative credit reports and poor references which will cause greater difficulty for people finding housing in the future. The union should not encourage people to break their promises and cause hardship on others. That is morally and ethically wrong. There are many positive ways the union can support people through these challenging times. This Rent Strike is anything but positive and is in fact, hurtful.

Another faculty member adds the middle-class liberal position:

> Renter doesn't pay landlord.
> Landlord doesn't pay mortgage servicer.
> Mortgage servicer does not make payment to investors in mortgage-backed securities.

> Who might one of those investors in MBS be? Blank, our own pension system.
> Blank loses income, so college and employees must increase contributions to keep Blank properly funded.
>
> We want our pensions guaranteed without burdensome additional contributions on our part. We also want to keep jobs, which means lightening the budgetary burden on the District. I would not be surprised if some of us who sign the Rent Strike Petition also demand that Blank achieve higher returns on investment to maintain proper funding without increasing employees and the District's contributions. Well, for Blank to satisfy us, they will demand that mortgage servicer make steady payments on the MBS, then mortgage servicer demands that landlord make payments, and then landlord puts the squeeze on tenants. Indirectly, we are just as responsible for the tenant ending up in the street, unless of course we are content to see Blank on rocky ground like other defined-benefit retirement funds.
>
> As long as our pensions, student loans, car loans, housing and other elements of social well-being are bound up with financialization/securitization of debt, none of us can claim complete innocence. As someone already implied, the problem faced by tenants is part of a broader problem associated with financial capitalism, late capitalism, or whatever you wish to call it.

Both full-time tenured faculty members essentially relay inherent structural class antagonisms as well as to imply where their own positions rest within the structure. First, the obviously conservative full-time tenured professor defends their class status and privilege via the "hard work pays off" argument that defies objective data and disregards economic theory. The more interesting response comes from the liberal full-time tenured professor who articulates the inherent structural contradictions that not only allows for impotence in combatting capitalism, but also mandates impotence. The liberal full-time tenured professor can do nothing else but articulate the classism of the structure. As usual with liberals of the middle class, the faculty member moralizes the situation by stating that "none of us can claim complete innocence." Notions of innocence or guilt are completely irrelevant. Whether full-time tenured faculty represent the cutthroat conservative moral and ethical attitudes of the former or the pseudo-empathetic moral and ethical attitudes of the latter, the objective reality of class distinction and its objective consequences, such as the inability for folks of the working class to pay rent, remains.

Course scheduling reveals another aspect of the class divide within educational institutions. It is both widely reported and widely known that full-time tenured faculty receive preferential scheduling. In times of budget cuts, full-time tenured faculty retain their basic security, especially in public institutions. Part-time instructors lack basic job security in the best of times and lack it even more during budget crises. For instance, at a college in the Northwest, schedules were made for a summer semester and both full-time and part-time faculty received courses to teach. When it became apparent that budgets would not allow for all of the assigned course sections to remain, all of the courses assigned to part-time instructors were canceled while all of the courses assigned to full-time professors remained.

The fact that pay for summer courses goes above and beyond the guaranteed salary for full-time faculty adds further evidence of the structural classism and obscenity that arises within capitalist education. On top of this, the part-time faculty were not even told that they would be losing their summer courses. Rather, the courses, some of which were already filled with students, simply disappeared from their schedules. Several months later, a part-time instructor voiced their dismay over the previous summer scheduling and requested that full-time faculty donate the upcoming summer courses for part-time instructors. After the part-time instructor made their case, the room fell silent. Full-time professors did not want to hear about or respond to it and the other part-time instructors did not want to be punished for speaking out against the full-time professor who schedules the courses.

In cases like these of obvious class division between full-time and part-time faculty, it is important to avoid or to reduce the situation to basic alienation, e.g. workers alienated from each other. The structural antagonisms bear a far broader foundation based in class structure and antagonisms previous to alienation within the workplace. People of the middle class perpetually maintain their advantages from birth with secure housing, healthy food, clean air, highly rated schools, safe neighborhoods, little addiction and violence, bank accounts, credit, college savings, healthcare, nannies, tutoring, preschool, piano lessons, and so on. People of the middle class fulfil basic destinies that land them their fully expected full-time tenured track positions. Folks of the working class live a different destiny, and the few who overcome the lack of secure housing, healthy food, clean air, highly rated schools, etc. and actually complete the educational requirements to teach, live in a vertiginous and anxious world of deeply rooted insecurity because of the many years they lived lacking basic security. In other words, this is not simply basic alienation between workers in a workplace, but alienation between classes in society eventually manifested in the workplace.

All of this is compounded by the widespread nepotism, cronyism, and tokenism, all of which reveal a perpetuation of classism. One example comes from a state university in the southeast. The university advertised a full-time tenured faculty position and interviewed several candidates. The position did not get filled. One candidate received an email from one of the professors on the hiring committee that stated that the chosen candidate did not take the position and that the hiring process would soon start over. The member of the hiring committee called the candidate and explained how to compose their letter of application, what to include on the CV, and how to respond during the interview. Obviously, the member of the hiring committee broke every rule in the hiring process. Nonetheless, the candidate was extremely excited about the opportunity.

Eventually, the process commenced, and the candidate followed all of the instructions from the hiring committee member fully expecting to get the job. Despite the advice of the hiring committee member, the candidate did not get the job. Upon investigation, it turned out that a good friend of the hiring committee member, who was also a professor at a nearby state university, contacted the hiring committee member and encouraged them to hire a recent graduate from their PhD program. Subsequently, the recent graduate received the job. Incidentally, the friend of the hiring committee member chaired the recent graduate's dissertation project. In addition, according to the anonymous poster, these full-time tenured professors frequently present at conferences to discuss equity and fairness in education. These practices are common and in plain view as over and over again part-time faculty witness friends and family getting hired for full-time positions. In this case, the professor on the hiring committee topped their own unethical practice during the same hiring process!

Another common practice involves the careful composition of preferred requirements on job vacancy descriptions. Essentially, hiring committees, or sometimes just a department chair or dean, have already decided who will be hired in advance. Constructing the right job announcement helps to eliminate qualified candidates and create the appearance of a fair hiring process. In a particularly obscene example reported on an anonymous forum, a part-time instructor received an email, out of the blue, from the department chair requesting their CV. The department chair stated that they did not have a copy on file. The part-time instructor quickly emailed the department chair the CV.

Before the department chair requested the CV, a job announcement and description was posted outlining that the preferred requirements were a PhD in one discipline, plus at least a Master's degree in another discipline, current teacher *and* administration K-12 certifications in the state, plus bilingual abilities along with a host of other requirements that would make any candidate hyper-uniquely qualified.

The part-time instructor who received the email that requested their CV fulfilled every requirement on the job description. *After* the department chair received and reviewed the part-time instructor's CV, the job description changed to include one more requirement that effectively disqualified the part-time instructor. Not so coincidentally, the person hired for the job attended the same university and graduated from the same program at almost the same time as the department chair.

To make it even more demoralizing, the anonymous part-time instructor mentioned that the person hired was most obviously born and bred in the upper middle class while the part-time instructor, who was deliberately disqualified from the position, was born and bred in the working class. One union representative mentioned to the disqualified part-time instructor that hiring practices had actually improved at the institution. He stated that previously job announcements would appear and disappear within a week or two and that nobody would be made aware that a position had opened and that nobody knew a position had even opened until the new hire was publicly announced.

To stress the point, economic class usually predetermines employment in education. Those of the middle class carry the preexisting advantages to gain full-time employment. The most significant being their college education. People of the middle class have economic access to the highest ranked universities, which is then used as a determinant for the qualifications and value of a job candidate. Countless teenagers of the working class achieve academic success, only to find out they cannot afford to attend a highly ranked university. The teenager must either go into debt to pay the tuition and other costs or work while studying. Obviously, this creates a far more difficult situation for teenagers from the working class. If the teenager from the working class chooses an affordable college, then the degree does not measure up in value. If the teenager from the working class "decides" to go into debt, then the burden of repayment requires the same laborious toil expected of all adult folks of the working class. All of this presents concrete disadvantages without even mentioning the access to other educational resources at the disposal of the middle class, such as private tutoring, personalized test preparation, free time, professional entrance application assistance, and family and friends who already attended college and who can fill out forms, make phone calls, and help with entrance applications.

To return to employment and the advantages of the middle class, a graduate of a small low rated university in the Midwest, who could not secure full-time employment contacted one of their former professors, who was now the Dean at the aforementioned low rated university. The Dean stated a job is opening up in the department, but because of your degree, it's a longshot. In other words, the degree that the student received from the very university with the job opening was not good enough to get a job at the university. The low rated university served students of the working class with a very low tuition and many financial aid programs to attend, but its very accessibility diminished its value, highlighting that access and cost correlate with value. The more accessible and lower cost the university, the lower the value of the degree.

Class serves as the central determinant of employment in education through tokenism, as well. The previously mentioned upper middle-class person who secured the job in favor of the working-class person was both Hispanic and female. Again, this type of hiring occurs all over the country and while raising the number of Hispanic women to the ranks of professor certainly appears positive, these token hires usually come from the middle class, thereby maintaining the classist structure.

According to a professor in the Northeast, their educational institution posted pictures and biographies of the candidates for the new college president. One was a working-class Black woman. Another was a middle-class Hispanic man, and the third was a middle-class White woman. The biography of the Black woman included a vast background in activism and advocacy for the homeless, rent control, affordable housing, drug and alcohol rehab, and community healthcare while the biographies of the two middle-class candidates (let's just say) did not. Clearly the Black woman was not an officious mediocre bureaucrat, but rather a dynamic, selfless, and active community member engaged in real organizing that supported the working class. These facts about her character and activities effectively canceled out her potential selection for the position as president. The middle-class white woman's biography read like a conservative politician's letter of introduction for a position as an executive board member for Pepsi Co. The middle-class Hispanic man got the job. Just smart enough, just mediocre enough, and just enough of everything to be a token. Aside from the Hispanic man's blind allegiance to the status quo stood his friendship with members of the selection committee. Classism, tokenism, and cronyism were on his side.

Another college announced a full-time faculty position that eventually received almost five hundred applications. The college hired a relatively inexperienced "in-house" adjunct instructor who recently graduated with their Master's Degree from a local university. The hire caused a certain level of dismay within the college because many who had far more experience, far more education, and, overall, far more qualifications were overlooked. The fact that the new hire was an immediate relative of a high-ranking administrator elevated the level of dismay. Looking closely at the hire, they fit all of the categories virtually required to secure full-time employment in an educational institution:

1. Middle-Class Background (Classism)
2. Hispanic Woman (Tokenism)
3. Friends with Current Admin. and Faculty (Cronyism)
4. Immediate Relative to a high-ranking Administrator (Nepotism)

Again, class functions as the central determinant of employment potential. If an educational institution needs to hire a person of an "underrepresented group," the token hire will be chosen from the middle class of the "underrepresented group." If the educational institution has its required number of token people from an "underrepresented group" then cronyism and nepotism play a key role in selecting who from the middle class will get the job. If tokenism, cronyism, and nepotism do not come into play, the candidate comes from the middle class. Bear in mind that departments can utilize cronyism and nepotism while being made up of a majority of people from "underrepresented groups." For instance, many colleges have almost entire departments made up of people from either one specific "underrepresented group" or a diverse range of people from "underrepresented groups." This creates a picture where there exists an appearance of diversity, but this somewhat faux diversity always lacks any significant representation of the working class.

Real Actual Interview:

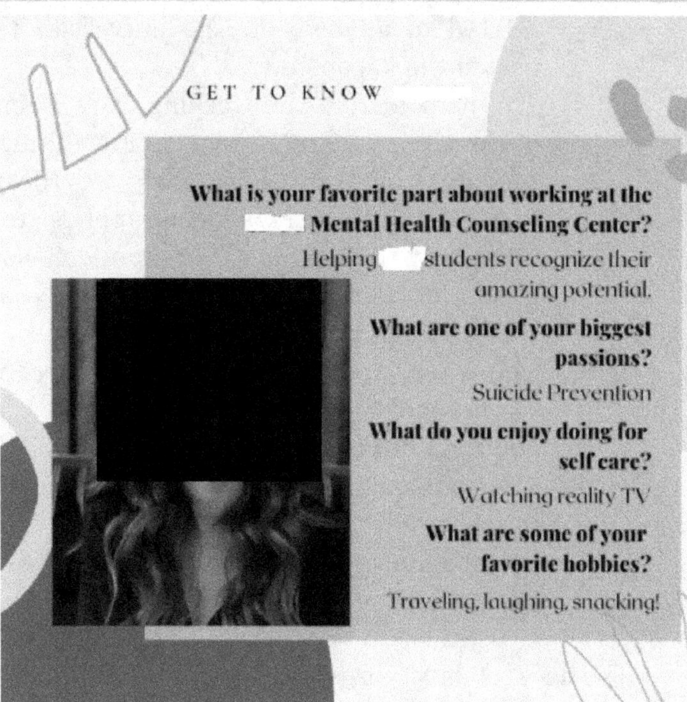

The rarest of all hiring scenarios:

1. Full-time tenure track professor job is posted by a university
2. A person from the working class who received their education at a university

accessible to the working class applies for the job.

3. The person from the working class does not know anybody at the university and is not related to anybody at the university that posted the job opening.
4. The person from the working class is most obviously of a race or ethnicity predetermined as unnecessary for the job (e.g. a White person who applies to a university that needs a token professor or a person of color who applies to a university that does not need a token professor).
5. The person from the working class receives correspondence from the hiring university about an interview for the position.
6. The person from the working class is interviewed.
7. The person from the working class receives a job offer and accepts the job.

The lack of labor organization and actual things labor can do to make this scenario possible underlies, in part, the predicament of folks of the working class in education. In short, many educational workers do not have a union and in places where they do have a union, the union is either virtually impotent or most obviously favors the tenured faculty of the middle class. Therefore, unionization, itself, does little to combat the classism within education. When one part-time union representative was asked why the part-time faculty does not organize separately from the full-time faculty he emphasized that part-time labor simply has no power to negotiate. When asked about going on strike, he noted that it is illegal. He then explained all of the laws, rules, statutes, regulations, and so forth that make any meaningful organized action of both part-time and full-time laborers impossible. In other words, it is structurally impossible to organize any meaningful action under past and current union agreements (or concessions), which relegates union representation to basic symbolic functions, e.g. the existence of the union as a goal and an end, itself.

Another part-time union representative noted that:

> Unfortunately, our union leadership for the last 20 years has been oriented towards serving the needs of full-timers. Solidarity? The [union] uses a veneer of progressive politics to cover up the goal of every contract negotiated, which is to extract the surplus labor of adjuncts and divide it between bloated administrators and full-time faculty. The question for me is how to present their hypocrisy in a way that doesn't just shut them out completely? I haven't been very successful at that.

This veneer of progressive politics coupled with its lack of interest or dedication to actual structural economic change typifies the liberal position of the middle class inside and outside of education. This could not be more evidenced than in the faculty, union, and administration support of Black Lives Matter, a group that fits firmly into capitalism with goals of inclusion, access, and social equality rather than specific goals against capitalism or objective changes to the economic structure. This is why BLM can so seamlessly integrate into the corporate promotional media sector (sports leagues, tech companies, etc.), unlike groups like the Black Panther Party or the League of Revolutionary Black Workers that could inherently, because of their politics, never do.

The more important point is that liberals of the middle-class support of BLM highlights how easy it is to sacrifice nothing but maintain a veneer of support for their soft version of something they call equity. Aside from the fact that BLM is, more or less (at least tacitly), a pro-capitalist group, liberals of the middle class have no ability to see their economic privilege as a direct cause of Black poverty and that structural change to the economic system will necessitate an overt sacrifice of their own economic or class status. Adam Curtis eloquently asserts:

> People who are the sort of the center of society at the moment . . . they would have a lot to lose from real political change because it really would change things in the structure of power . . . or [these are the brutal questions]: Do you just want things to change a little bit? Do you just want the banks to be a little bit nicer or people to be a little more respectful of each other's identities? All of which is good, but basically you carry on living in your nice world where you tinker with it. There are millions of people out there who want change and the key thing is . . . you might have lots to lose, but they feel they've got absolutely nothing to

> lose. [...] The forgotten thing about politics is that you give up some of your individualism to something bigger than yourself; you surrender yourself . . . ***you can spot real change happening when you see people from the liberal middle class beginning to give themselves up to something*** [and] surrender themselves for something bigger. At the moment there is nothing like that in the liberal imagination.[5]

Within education, those at the center of the system aim to maintain their class status because they do, in fact, have a lot to lose. The liberal imagination, or lack thereof, permits them to discern what aspects of educational policy allows for safe tinkering, but avoids any real change. Liberal administrators and full-time faculty comfortably promote diversity, equity, and the like because it exemplifies tinkering with no significant sacrifice. The bigger economic changes, liberatory and revolutionary, that might produce actual changes to the structure of power requires an overcoming or a surrender of the self in favor of the collective good for those with nothing to lose.

A central problem that exists which contributes to the lack of middle-class sacrifice involves the horizon of change. BLM offers very little in terms of mass structural changes, especially ones that lie outside of the capitalist mode of production and its discourse. The "defunding" of the police illustrates how even the solutions to the problem of police brutality and profiling and its disproportionate targeting of Black folks rest within capital, e.g. give the police less money to operate; but they do not aim to alter the underlying economic base that produces the necessity to commit crimes, which requires policing. The inclusion of more Black folks into the middle class does not attack the economic base that produces Black poverty. It just shifts proportions and keeps the capitalist mode of production in place. This explains the support of people from the middle class for BLM and other policies, attitudes, and reforms where the limited horizon for change exists within capitalist discourse. The middle class simply do not have to sacrifice themselves, but rather they can maintain their class status and allow for the entrance of a few "underrepresented" folks into their class.

BLACK
LIVES
MATTER

VOTE

LOVE IS LOVE
SCIENCE IS REAL
BLACK LIVES MATTER
WE ARE ALL IMMIGRANTS
IS FOR EVERYONE
KINDNESS IS EVERYTHING

BLACK
LIVES
MATTER

BLACK
LIVES
MATTER

Perhaps we exist in what Baudrillard calls a "post-orgy" society where horizons for change have simply been absorbed into capitalism and continue as symbols of a foreclosed history. Maybe the answer to his question from 1986 has been answered:

> On the aromatic hillsides of Santa Barbara, the villas are all like funeral homes. Between the gardenias and the eucalyptus trees, among the profusion of plant genuses and the monotony of the human species, lies the tragedy of a Utopian dream made reality. In the very heartland of wealth and liberation, you always hear the same question: 'What are you doing after the orgy?' What do you do when everything is available - sex, flowers, the stereotypes of life and death? This is America's problem and, through America, it has become the whole world's problem.[6]

The period of global orgies (liberation movements, social and political rights, workers' rights, the vote, sexual liberation, the rights of women, gender equality and so on) emancipated so much in an orgasmic burst of energy (*jouissance*) but now exist within the confines of a constantly flowing over-saturation and over-signification of solipsistic self-referential idealism. Global orgies have turned into pseudo-collective masturbation. "Join the orgy by masturbating!" "Welcome to the orgy, now masturbate!" The middle class imagine themselves in the midst of an orgy while they masturbate. Just as "self-improvement is masturbation," inclusion is masturbation for the middle class. It is a safe space where desire comes protected with condoms (structural regulations, laws, rules, statutes, policies) for masturbation. "Join the orgy, but you must wear a condom while you jerk yourself off!" As Debord says this is "the ruling order's nonstop discourse about itself, its never-ending monologue of self-praise, [and] its self-portrait at the stage of totalitarian domination of all aspects of life."[7] It is the middle class talking to themselves about race, gender, equity, equality, mindfulness, and diversity as they point to their own obsessions with micro-aggressions and implicit biases through a self-absorbed self-aggrandizement where privilege implies their own privilege, class implies their own status and indicates their own denial of a material reality that exists independent of them and a denial of objective knowledge outside of their enclosure, all of which facilitates the mirrored monologue in their own paradoxical masturbatory orgasm.[8]

In education, it is the innumerable array of faculty and staff professional development trainings that exhaust every aspect of the introspective liberalism from the middle class within the matrix of mindfulness. None of which ever address the concrete conditions of class structure. In the post-orgy society, Baudrillard presents a "Forth World" where "entire social groups are being laid waste from the inside" and that "society has forgotten them."[9] Now they are "zombies condemned to obliteration, consigned to statistical graphs of endangered species. This is the Fourth World. Entire sectors of our modern societies, entire countries in the Third World now fall into this Fourth World desert zone. But whereas the Third World still had a political meaning, the Fourth World has none." Baudrillard finally laments, "Nothing will be done to save them and perhaps nothing can be done, since enfranchisement, emancipation, and expansion have already taken place [the orgy]."[10] Folks from the working class live as these zombies and exist only as statistics or in over-identified micro-sectors in society (not as objective exploited economic classes, but as specifically defined oppressed subjective identities that exist in every strata of economic class).

Harmony Korine's 1997 film *Gummo* offers a glimpse into a Forth World zone that avoids the heavy handed middle and upper middle-class moralism found in most films about poverty.[11] It profoundly reveals the mental distress, poor physical health, violence, homophobia, substance abuse, domestic abuse, sexual abuse, incest, and racism that predominately exists in spaces inhabited by folks of the working class. The film does not noble-ize the demoralizing effects of poverty. It presents images that exist in the objective reality of half of the population of the United States.

The real tornado that destroyed the city of Xenia, OH, the setting of the film, serves as the underlying metaphor of the destruction of a working-class industrial town. Filmed and released in the 1990s, during and after the tornado of neoliberal capitalism destroyed towns like Xenia, the film begins with a scene of a teenage couple who sit in a 1970s smashed up automobile (deindustrialization) in a junk yard and are about to kiss. When the teen feels up the girl's breast he discovers a lump or the cancer that infiltrates each aspect of postindustrial working-class America (not to mention the lack of access to healthcare and the unhealthy living conditions, such as unhealthy air, water, food, etc.). The Forth World, entirely forgotten, as towns and cities were systematically decimated.[12] The decimation exists in plain sight. It is on the other side of the tracks or in the darkness on the edge of town. It is in Xenia, OH and innumerable other towns and cities. The main character of *Gummo*, Tummler, summarizes *being* in the Fourth World:

> Dear world, I have confusion around me in every direction from my brain. I've tried and tried to make it here in this fucking world, but I think it was a mistake that I was ever born. I do not feel guilty about taking my own life. I've tried your ways. I've had a job since I was thirteen years old. Making a living was never a real problem for me. The problem was all I see is misery and darkness. Die, die, die. I'll put a gun to my fucking head right now. I'm so pissed I could kill you, But I'm not going to.[13]

Does Tummler need a positive attitude? Perhaps Tummler should meditate or do yoga. If only Tummler could practice mindfulness, he could see the world differently. Tummler and his friend Solomon kill cats and sell the meat to a local grocer who then sells the meat to the Chinese restaurant denoting the black market capitalism within a desolate community. The cats offer a supply of fresh meat for exploitation, just let them reproduce and grow to maturity, then exploit them as nothing more than a commodity in the marketplace (exemplified by the "Rabbit Boy" character). With the money from selling cats, Tummler and Solomon buy glue to sniff in order to escape their predicament via an altered mindset or a version of meditation for the American working class.

Meditation in the Fourth World:

The movie culminates in a scene that illustrates the class divide between the middle class and the working class. Three young working-class sisters hand out flyers in an attempt to find their missing cat (which was killed) and run into a middle-class man who tells them he has their missing cat. He gets the girls to ride in his car and attempts to molest them. As they scream at him and rebuff his advances he yells back at them several times, "You're ho's anyway. It's no big deal. It's nothing new for trash like you."[14] This scene illustrates how there exists an inherent perspective of the working class by the middle class. This perspective is that working-class folks are worthless trash who, like animals, are there to be exploited.

This gets back to the paradoxical trap of responsibilization that the middle class impose upon the working class. Fisher encapsulates it: "A population that has all its life been sent the message that it is good for nothing is simultaneously told that it can do anything it wants to do."[15] Near the end of the film Tummler whispers, "Life is beautiful. Really it is. Full of beauty and illusions. Life is great. Without it, you'd be dead."[16] His hope and the hope of the working class resides in the fact that without life is death. Being alive is better than being dead, but the prospect of death helps to maintain life. As French Psychoanalyst Jacques Lacan once said, "Death belongs to the realm of faith. You're right to believe you will die. It sustains you. If you didn't believe it, how could you bear the life you have? If we couldn't rely on the total certainty that it will end, how could you bear all this?"[17] Tummler lives with the mental trauma inherent in the working class within the capitalist mode of production. He must erect a façade of beauty and illusions in order to defend against this trauma. Life is the reason to remain alive and nothing more.

According to Curtis, the Tummlers and Solomons of the world (the Fourth World residents), or those "who feel they have nothing to lose, are being led by the [political] right"[18] who manufacture another set of beauty and illusions like nationalism, patriotism, and ethnic heritage. Liberals of the middle class, both inside and outside of education, who have a lot to lose, appear to consider the potential revolutionary character of those being led by the political right as merely a challenge to democracy. Liberals of the middle class want to keep the democracy of capitalism, which carries no potential for revolutionary change and is entirely embedded in global neoliberalism. As the mainstream left aims to maintain neoliberalism, the right becomes more embolden to attack every sector of society. An underclass of the Fourth World, radicalized by the illusions of the political right, may veer toward revolutionary activity.

This is a problem for the liberals of the middle class and has its origins that date back to the 1960s. Phil Ochs perfectly explains this problem in his song "Love Me, I'm a Liberal."

> I go to civil rights rallies
> And I put down the old D.A.R.
> I love Harry and Sidney and Sammy
> I hope every colored boy becomes a star
> But don't talk about revolution
> That's going a little bit too far
> So love me, love me, love me, I'm a liberal[19]

The liberal imagination of the middle class cannot envision revolution. They cannot imagine that the reactionary right thinks of revolution. It continues to support the politics of proportion and inclusion into capitalism rather than to support revolutionary change that may actually result in real racial and economic security. Its central strategy, inside and outside of education, to maintain capitalism, revolves around privileging internal subjective individualist solutions that preserve the underlying objective conditions that cause racial and economic problems. Mindfulness is not liberatory nor revolutionary, but only the internal illusions of the liberal middle class. There may be a revolution on the horizon as Ochs sings:

> And the soft middle class crowded in to the last,
> For the building was fully surrounded.
> And the noise outside was the ringing of revolution.
> As the windows were smashed by the ringing of revolution.
> Down on our knees we're begging you please,
> We're sorry for the way you were driven.
> There's no need to taunt just take what you want,
> And we'll make amends, if we're living.
> But away from the grounds the flames told the town
> That only the dead are forgiven.
> As they crumbled inside the ringing of revolution.[20]

Except it will not be the revolution that Ochs describes that comes from an armed group of multiracial folks of the working class led by the radical political left. Rather the revolution will come from an armed group of reactionary (pseudo)fascist folks (many of whom are of the working class) led by the radical political right. As long as liberals of the middle class dominate the politics of the left with its overt omission of or interest in economic class as a means of organizing or as a focus of direct political action, the potential for the reactionary right to expand political activity and influence exists.

Therefore, the working class must aim to seize not only the means of production, but also the educational system to enforce a revolutionary working-class education. Education can no longer be controlled by the middle class who clearly and consistently do not support the goals or even the interests of the working class (even internally). They may, by a certain definition, share the interests of the working class because they do not own any means of production, but organizing with them has been and will continue to be fruitless. Essentially it is time to forget the liberals of the middle class in the fight for working-class revolutionary change. Inside educational institutions, the working class must act by taking over, perhaps by force, administrator and full-time faculty spaces. Students of the working class must reject the education of the middle class and demand an education that eliminates ideas foregrounded by mindfulness and subjective change that focuses on American Dream motifs of hard work and merit. Every classroom should revolve around changing the objective material conditions of the capitalist world.

[1] Noam Chomsky and Edward Herman, *Manufacturing Consent: The Political Economy of Mass Media*, 2 & 304.

[2] Class consciousness occurs in two ways, unconsciously and consciously. The great majority of people in both the middle and working class are unconsciously conscious of their class. This point of the old joke from Žižek about Rumsfeld's "unknown knowns." https://www.youtube.com/watch?v=ql80Klk4pSU.

People confront material obligations or the set of predetermined activities and behaviors that determine the "knowns," but are unaware of how these "knowns" determine their being in the world. If we follow Freire and critical pedagogies, educators would aim to turn these "unknown knowns" into "known knowns" through finding both "known unknowns" and "unknown unknowns" via critical thinking. Once the student or whomever identifies these "known unknowns" and "unknown unknows" they can also identify their "unknown knowns." The problem with this is that "unknown knowns" develop from the material obligations or the set of predetermined activities and behaviors. Therefore, those must be changed in order to change the "unknown knowns." Freire and critical pedagogues are doing it backwards. They think that changing the mind first will lead to people to change the material obligations or the set of predetermined activities and behaviors.

[3] Mark Fisher "Good for Nothing" March 19, 2014.

[4]https://www.latimes.com/local/lanow/la-me-ln-citizens-academy-20180323-htmlstory.html, Brittney Meija, "Many Latinos answer call of the Border Patrol in the age of Trump," April 23, 2018.

[5] Chapo Trap House: Episode 65 - No Future feat. Adam Curtis, 2016, https://www.youtube.com/watch?v=G04VHfc0llg.

[6] Jean Baudrillard, *America*, 30.

[7] Guy Debord, *The Society of the Spectacle*, 7.

[8] Actually excerpt from an email: "Join educators across the state in this intentional space to practice mindful breathing, reflective journaling, and heart sharing."

[9] Baudrillard, *America*, 112-113.

[10] Ibid., 113.

[11] *Gummo*, Harmony Korine, Fine Line Features, 1997.
[12] See Jefferson Cowie's book *Stayin' Alive: The 1970s and the Last Days of the Working Class.*
[13] *Gummo*, Harmony Korine, Fine Line Features, 1997.
[14] Ibid.
[15] https://theoccupiedtimes.org/?p=12841, Mark Fisher, "Good for Nothing," March 19, 2014.
[16] *Gummo*, Harmony Korine, Fine Line Features, 1997.
[17] "Lacan on Death," https://www.youtube.com/watch?v=EW2F8WtruAY
[18] Chapo Trap House: Episode 65 - No Future feat. Adam Curtis 2016, https://www.youtube.com/watch?v=G04VHfc0llg.
[19] Phil Ochs, Lyrics to "Love me, I'm a Liberal," https://genius.com/Phil-ochs-love-me-im-a-liberal-lyrics
[20] Phil Ochs, Lyrics to "Ringing of Revolution," https://genius.com/Phil-ochs-ringing-of-revolution-lyrics

Chapter 7: Teach: Policing, Competition, Individualism, Hard Work, Capitalism and Class, & Communication

Policing

There exists several types of policing, both formal and informal. Educators must teach against all forms of policing. The formal agencies, such as Police & Sheriff's Departments, Border Patrol, ICE, and the Military must be challenged. First of all, educators must dismiss the "bad apple" ideology. Rather, educators must challenge the policing institutions and not individuals or small groups within these policing agencies. Only under very specific material circumstances can any of these agencies appear to benefit the wellbeing of the public. One can see this in the arguments that support policing agencies, such as the robbery argument, e.g. someone wants to rob your home! Or the global terrorism argument, e.g. terrorists want to change your religion! Or the anti-immigration argument, e.g. immigrants smuggle, rape, and take your jobs! All three of these examples exist only within a very specific material framework, such as a class structured, Christian, Nationalistic, capitalist society. Obviously, these arguments, based in emotion, touch people whose concrete circumstances result in the belief in these values, but all of these arguments exist within a distinct time and place and make policing appear necessary. Educators may attack these arguments, but that does not directly challenge policing as an institution and allows for contextualized counterarguments, like the three above.

For example, students from the working class, many from nonwhite populations, may have parents who police for wages, whether it be the Border Patrol, ICE, local police, or the Military. In fact, folks from the working class commonly work in the branches of professional policing. In many cases, these working-class folks who police display and manifest all the characteristics of "good citizens" and/or "good people." A student may say, "My father goes to church and coaches my sister's softball team. He would never shoot an unarmed Black person." Countless arguments that sound reasonable support folks who police and that makes it difficult to argue against policing. This requires educators to conceptualize policing as a group of institutions with a set of very specific objectives (e.g. protecting private property, opening new markets, keeping markets open, etc.) rather than individuals who sometimes protect ordinary people and freedoms. Therefore, policing must be taken out of the dominant American context that rationalizes policing. In other words, for all of the harmful things policing institutions do, they also do things that, because of the objective crime in American society, appear to prevent harmful things. For example, in a nation riddled with crime, such as the U.S., some policing appears justified. The idea is to trace the root causes of crime and eliminate those, thus, eliminating the need for the massive and militarized policing agencies. Therefore, mass policing would be objectively illegitimate and illogical in a nation without very much crime. Get rid of the reasons people commit crime; get rid of the crime; get rid of the police.

The prevention of crime appears as a valid argument within the context of the contemporary United States. Henceforth, educators must consider the underlying causes of crime. What makes people commit crimes? What type of crimes are being committed? Much of the crime is related to private property ownership, such as theft of private property. People steal because they need money and other resources to survive. People need money because they are objectively poor. The U.S. has 50 million poor people, but the data is a bit misleading. To be considered officially impoverished means a yearly income of $25,465 or less for a family with two adults and two children.[1] So the actual number of impoverished people, based in real wages, is more like 100 million people. But if we consider economic insecurity, such as living paycheck to paycheck, we have 75%-80% of the population.[2] Most people are poor or economically insecure in the U.S. Thus, people commit property crime.

Aside from some sort of theft (robbery, larceny, car theft, burglary), which constitutes most crime in the US, violent crime stems from poverty, such as the mass proliferation of crime within black market economies. Folks of the working class have little hope or choice in the matter. The choice is essentially what sector of the black market economy will one choose: drugs, guns, human trafficking, etc. In short, all of this must be policed. So police disproportionately police poor and/or propertyless people. As long as we have private property, we have poverty and general economic insecurity. As long as we have poverty and general economic insecurity, we have police. This is across the spectrum of race. For instance, the number of people shot and killed by police in 2020 (the numbers remain fairly consistent year to year) are: 2020 Police Killings: African-Americans 226; Hispanics 156; Whites 432.[3]

Just about all of the people killed by police are of the working class and do not own private property. The point is that unless we make a commitment to eliminate poverty and private property ownership, we will have crime and policing. What is worse is that policing can be safely justified because *crime is an objective fact.* A quick search for global data on crime highlights how nations with less poverty or more evenly distributed wealth have less crime and, subsequently, less policing. Educators must teach this fact. Regardless, private property equals poverty, which equals crime, and crime equals policing.

This holds true internationally. The United States, essentially, mass produces dangerous weapons, sells them internationally, and proclaims that the world is a dangerous place. Then, they ship off the military to police the world after arming it.

The role of the military incorporates the same role as domestic police: protect private property, keep markets open, and open new markets. Somehow, this entire business enterprise has become a reason for adoration. Whether it is in media, local schools, or at church, the adoration of global policing now infiltrates each moment of American life. Salutes to the military proliferate and criticizing this form of global policing and subsequent violence elicits surprise and sometimes anger from others. Nothing could be more obvious than the fact that the U.S. military is a violent policing institution, yet every possible mass public moment must include admiration for this violence.

Like the domestic police, most of the military includes folks from the working class with many from nonwhite populations. Like domestic policing, they join for a wage. Therefore, the military is not made up of patriots who aim to serve their country, but rather, folks of the working class who need a job. Since the intensified union busting and the end of U.S. manufacturing that began in the 1970s, workers cannot simply go to a factory or a mine and make a decent wage with benefits and retirement as they could in the post WW2 period. This means that entire generations of working-class folks join policing forces for economic survival. The working class has become the policing class. Formerly, it produced the world's goods and now it protects the private property and market interests of those who displaced and decimated it. This goes beyond wage slavery and into a real crisis of classism. Truthfully, joining the military offers real objective and material benefits to the working class of all races, but it also represents a form of barbarity that mirrors the days when capitalists would send children down into mines. Instead of mines, they send the military to the desert or elsewhere into dangerous territory to be maimed or killed in service to global capitalism. Just as children sacrificed their lives in mines for capitalism, present day folks of the working class sacrifice their lives for capitalism. The only difference is in the public relations.

The troops are made of folks from the working class, the (slight) majority of whom come from nonwhite populations. Educators who teach military or ex-military students report the same data: most join for a job, and many suffer from mental distress. One instructor of military and ex-military students notes that every single semester several military students compose essays about the alcoholism, depression, and suicide in the military.[4] Folks of the working class suffer disproportionately from mental distress and entrance into the military exacerbates the already common distresses among the working class.

Many wonder why those with the least will police for the interests of those with the most. As mentioned, people do it for a wage, but this does not explain why some folks from the working class police with dedication, energy, enthusiasm, and passion, as if they were policing to serve their own class interests. More distressing is the fact that nonwhite folks from the working class will directly police against their own racial interests with dedication, energy, enthusiasm and passion. Educators must recognize this fact and use it to inform their understanding of policing. There are countless domestic examples to share of working-class Whites who police working-class Whites and working-class Blacks who police working-class Blacks and working-class Hispanics who police working-class Hispanics. There are also countless international examples of working-class Blacks who police working-class Africans and working-class Hispanics who police working-class Central Americans, etc. This policing only serves the interest of rich property owning, profit driven capitalists. Of course, people of all races police people of all races, which is why organizing for economic change around race presents very specific problems. But to get back to the main point, why would some people of the working class enthusiastically and passionately police for the bourgeoisie with such energy and dedication?

One possible explanation points to the material structure of hierarchal arrangements and the roles of people within them. Generally, when one enters a certain role they must take on all of the objective functions of that particular role. For example, all educators can quickly recall the teacher who becomes an administrator and essentially becomes a different person. The shift of the person does not initially come from some internal shift of ideas or attitude, but rather from the concrete dictates of the new role. All must fulfill the concrete requirements of any professional role, which subsequently, alters their ideas and attitudes. In some cases, the role takes on the entire foundation or reason for being, (they live for their jobs). Imagine a person from the working class who comes from an impoverished environment full of crime and insecurity. Then, imagine this person getting a uniform and the duty to serve and protect. Class and race become secondary to the uniform and the duty. More significantly, in terms of domestic policing, policing involves the policing of the very people who live in the impoverished environment full of crime and insecurity. So it becomes the duty of some folks of the working class to police other folks of the working class. There is a definite distinction between the two groups (those who police vs. those who must be policed). This distinction creates the conflict between the police and the community. The people who newly police change roles and change perspectives on poverty and insecurity, as a result of the newly required duty. Individually, the idea becomes "I must fulfill my duty in this uniform." The more dedicated to the role, the more evident the distinction.

Along with the duty comes detailed policies that support the role. Policing becomes a role that hides behind policies, procedures, protocols, and rules which further exacerbates the distinction between people within the same class and/or race. These policies enable the "Just doing my job" or "Just following the protocol" or "Just obeying the orders" excuse. They create a gap between people of the same class and race. This also makes it possible to embrace the role that directly conflicts with the class and racial interests of those who police. It blurs the gap or makes the gap invisible. The much more obvious gap involves class, itself. Those who police receive a steady wage and so forth. Policing institutions always need police and hire constantly (budget being the only factor that prevents hiring). If one wants a job policing, one can get a job policing. This is especially true for the military. They are ALWAYS hiring. But once inside the institution of policing, there comes the internal competition for promotions, incentives, awards, and so forth. Policing includes the same sort of worker alienation that any other job includes. Thus, some work to be the best police they can be. To be the best police they can be, they must *be* the role of police officer and, structurally, there are no built in considerations for class and/or racial allegiance. In fact, the structure informs class and/or racial antagonisms and eliminates class and/or racial allegiance.

Obviously, there exists a spectrum of individual beliefs and attitudes toward class and race within policing institutions (and individuals who police), but the material structure (fulfilling the duty of the role) overwhelms any sort of beliefs or attitudes about class and race. Incredibly, some assert that a more racially diverse police force will result in a more equitable form of policing! This absurdity follows the same logic that a more diverse corporate executive board will result in a more equitable form of business practice. In both cases, the diversity of the policing force or the diversity of the executive board matters little because, structurally, the police must police (protect private property, keep markets open, and open new markets) and the corporation must make profit (exploit workers, etc.). Neither of them structurally aim toward economic change. Therefore, when educators teach policing, they must focus on the structure of policing (domestic police, Border Patrol, the military, other Federal and State Agencies, etc.) and how it operates within the context of a capitalist system both domestically and internationally.

Individualism

Individualism represents a cornerstone of capitalism and dominates the material structure of society, which in turn, dominates the ideological framework of capitalist societies. Concepts of individualism feature in the entire political spectrum from far-right to far-left. This makes it difficult to challenge notions of individualism in the setting of education. By default, students enter the classroom valuing individualism and educators reinforce this value through their teaching practice. Through emphasizing individuality, educators (perhaps unconsciously) reinforce the very dictates of capitalism that produce the basis of our competitive and divisive world.[5]

Students always reflect the ideology of the material capitalist structure and educators must directly combat this reflection. Some educators suggest to initiate critical thinking among the students with the hope that students can independently think their way out of capitalist ideology. This is not the best method.

Tim Gunn and a Leaky Shower

An interesting example comes from a very brief narrative written by Maggie Downs called "Tim Gunn and a Leaky Shower: Welcome to my Life, Little Guy."[6] The narrative revolves around the plights of a new mother who suffers in her sweltering hot apartment slum with her newborn son while undocumented workers repair her shower. Out of desperation she binge watches the reality television show *Project Runway* whose host, Tim Gunn, advises the contestants to "Make it work!" Students (and probably instructors) *always* understand this narrative foregrounded by the capitalist concept of individualism. Students will respond by writing something similar to the following:

> After reading this essay it made me think of the strength of a woman. With all that she had going on around her, she still managed to hold on and pull things together. That's how I remember my Mom and Grandmothers being when I was younger. They definitely knew how to "make it work." Ensuring that

> we had what we needed and were properly taken care of.
>
> My conclusion on reading this essay is that when life gets tough and things aren't the way you want them to be you need to fix them and make them better.
>
> I like the "make it work" method. I can remember when I was trying so hard to make everything perfect for my father, everything seemed to blown out of proportion. Making sure supper was on the table, babies fed, bathed, and put to bed, laundry out on the line, etc. keeping up with everything was incredibly challenging. I learned that I had to "make it work."
>
> Through all of the construction and weeks it took for repairs, I only wonder why the husband did not take more of a role or why was the landlord not contacted? This narrative is a realistic approach about how we experience obstacles in our lives, and we have to overcome them. We can overcome obstacles when focused, and we put our minds to it. Think about challenges you have had in the past, obstacles you had to face, were you able to overcome them?

As illustrated above, students focus on the individual will of the protagonist to overcome obstacles. They also refer to the individual decision to contact the landlord and solicit help from the husband. The narrative clearly states that the "landlady" is a slumlord and that the husband is at work. Although students mention the issue of gender, they never mention the issue of class.

Students fail to understand the narrative in terms of the community or the society. They always individualize Downs' situation and agree or identify with the tough love, "Make it work!" approach. In essence, they see themselves as individuals who must individually overcome obstacles in life, by default. They fail to see that life does not have to be a series of obstacles to be overcome individually. Of course, this ideological perspective emerges from the material conditions in which they reside.

Downs' situation in the narrative highlights how the material conditions inform her behavior and that the allowable or even conceivable decisions circulate around how the individual will deal with the material conditions. The striking aspect of her context involves the complete lack of a community around her. It simply does not exist. Things that would most definitely support a new mother that can easily be mandated and funded through public resources and supplied by the local community, such as child care centers, home child care support, paid paternal leave, temporary housing (with a working shower and working air condition), and so on simply do not exist as material conditions or possibilities in Maggie Downs' world nor in the real world. She is left with no alternative but to "Make it work!"

Aside from "Make it work!" students only suggest that her husband, family, or friends should offer help. They never suggest the state or the community, or any collective effort as a solution to Downs' issues. All of the students noble-ize her overcoming of her obstacles rather than offer any suggestion to change the actual material conditions which create her difficulties. It is Downs' character that is under analysis and never the system that generates the necessity for her to display the "strength" of character.

Furthermore, there is something a bit uneasy about Gunn's phrase "Make it work!" and the concept of *Project Runway*, in general. For instance, "Make it work" fits with the concrete material reality and dominant ideology of the individual as maker of one's destiny. In other words, if *you* didn't make it work, then *you* are to blame for not making it work. Gunn represents an authority figure who serves as a dictatorial critic of the individual worker who must compete against other workers to keep the job. Again, this also firmly fits in with the concrete material reality and dominant ideology of American capitalism. *Project Runway* serves as a TV microcosm of life in capitalism. The contestants are stressed out, overworked, and disposable within the system of production. If one fails, another can replace the failure in a moment's time. Gunn is the boss who represents the technician of the system, like a machine. There is no space for morality, sympathy, or empathy to emerge. His job is to critique, demand, and dispose. No excuses, just make it work.

This is a predicament for folks of the working class. The structure of the capitalist system does not include support for new mothers of the working class, such as day care centers, child care aides who come to the home, etc. The landlord carries no requirement to provide alternate housing for the tenant during repairs nor adequate air conditioning. Therefore, the new mother is left to

"Make it work!" on her own as an individual and her potential failure is hers and hers alone, despite the system that manufactures these circumstances for individuals. Or to put it another way, the system is structured to more likely produce failure than to produce success. If she does overcome these material obstacles then she is noble.

The problem does not exist exclusively with the students but also with educators who, because of immersion in the material structure of capitalism, tend to take the perspective of the noble individual. This permeates into pedagogy, in general.

American Psycho & Self-Care/Self-Love

The proliferation of self-care/self-love indicates that the elements of collective care and social love simply do not emerge from the capitalist mode of production. The hyper-focused attention on the "self" emerges from the lack of basic collective health and wellness care. If you are unhealthy or if you look unhealthy, it is your fault and your fault alone.

YouTube offers thousands of self-care/self-love videos to help individuals to look and feel great. Basically, the videos include things like morning routines, exercises, meditation, mindfulness, yoga, spas, and so on. They include descriptions of health commodities like lotions, soaps, creams, brushes, fabrics, sprays, and yoga mats. The videos also include people who describe the commodities they use for self-care/self-love and sometimes they share the excitement of opening the box with the audience (unboxing).

American Psycho, a novel written in the late 1980s by Bret Easton Ellis, obviously connects to this trend. What the main character, Patrick Bateman, clearly narrates hyperbolically, with the tedious and constant descriptions of consumer commodities and his own self-care/self-love routines, has hyper-intensified since the 1980s. What we see on YouTube includes a vast multitude of Patrick Batemans or American psychos. They *appear* to be from the middle class, and they create videos frighteningly similar to the opening scene of the film version of *American Psycho.* Clearly, Patrick Bateman represents the hyper-focused attention on the individual in capitalism and so do the YouTubers.[7]

Mark Fisher notes:

> There's no doubt that late capitalism certainly articulates many of its injunctions via an appeal to (a certain version of) health. But there are limits to this emphasis on good health: mental health and intellectual development barely feature at all, for instance. What we see instead is a reductive, hedonistic model of health which is all about 'feeling and looking good.'[8]

When questioned, most students will support the notion of self-care/self-love based in the logic of confidence. Students make statements that emphasize the confidence they feel when they focus on the hedonistic model of health, such as, "Branded clothing gives me confidence"; "Expensive makeup makes me feel more confident"; or "Looking fit gives me confidence." The lack of confidence draws attention to a general lack of basic security within the society. These examples go beyond simple consumerism. Rather, they expose the shallow nature of being that capitalism generates through a general insecurity in all dimensions of life whether social or economic. As Fisher claims, mental health and intellectual development play only slight roles in the nurturing of the self. Somehow educators connect the hedonistic model of health with mental and intellectual wellbeing by essentially correlating capitalist notions of feeling and looking good to higher achievement.

This borders on the concept of body image, which again, illustrates a lack in society. The lack, especially among youth, revolves around the social element of the self-care/self-love binary, e.g. looking and feeling bad. When one looks bad, one feels bad. When one feels bad, one must look bad. If one can look good, then one can feel good and if one can feel good, then one must look good. The deeper mental health issues which proliferate capitalist spaces dominated by the capitalist mode of production predetermine mental distress by default. Thus, the starting point for students is to feel bad. Then the self-care/self-love must commence. So, start to work out, diet, exercise, wear makeup, wear the right clothes, meditate, do yoga, be mindful, etc. All of these activities are individual, subjective, internal "feelings" that overcompensate for the lack in the social and economic structure to produce feeling good as the default mode of being.

American Psycho aptly conveys this solipsistic hyper-self-referential obsession with looking and feeling good. Bateman epitomizes the appearance of success in capitalism. He is upper middle class, good looking, dresses perfectly, and owns all the most advanced technological objects and latest commodities. He parties and socializes. Again, by all appearances, he is success. Somehow he developed a growth mindset. But the novel offers the other side of the spectrum of behavior which emerges as a necessity in capitalism: violence. Bateman kills homeless people, women, rivals, and anyone he pleases *and* without consequence. His appearance of success allows him to navigate through society without the fear of suffering any consequences. As a metaphor for capitalism, he highlights the lack of accountability of the capitalist corporate state. It can operate in plain sight as a source of obvious violence.

Self-care/self-love individualism perfectly complements the violence of capitalism. The violence of capitalism not only determines the material conditions for individualism (private property, for example), but is also served by the population who, whether consciously or unconsciously, promotes and perpetuates individualism. Bateman exists because everyone is or becomes Bateman and has little choice in being otherwise. The fact that self-care/self-love mainly emerges from liberal ideology highlights the detachment from social wellbeing the entire allowable spectrum of political thought produces. While Bateman is clearly conservative, although generally apolitical, his self-care/self-love healthy lifestyle fits perfectly into the liberalism of trendy and commodified Zen-organic mindful self-obsession. Thus, the violence can materialize within seemingly oppositional political modes. The Dead Kennedys' song "California Über Alles" most appropriately describes this dialectic:

> Zen fascists will control you
> Hundred percent natural
> You will jog for the master race
> And always wear the happy face

Žižek quotes the late Japanese Professor of Buddhist philosophies, Teitaro Suzuki:

> When I try to kill some of you it is really not me, but the sword itself that does the killing, he (the killer) has no desire to do harm to anybody but the enemy appears and makes himself a victim, it is although the sword performs automatically its function of justice which is the function of mercy.[9]

There is no Patrick Bateman; he is just an abstraction. The cool detachment nurtured through hyper-attention to the internal subjective individual allows for the detachment from violence. The military machinery, the industrial prison complex, and mass exploitation of global labor are all external to the individual. You be you. You do you. The individual can detach as a perpetrator of institutional violence and as a victim of institutional violence. If everybody just cared and loved themselves . . .

Žižek overtly connects this to the capitalist modes of production. He writes:

> The 'Western Buddhist' meditative stance is arguably the most efficient way for us to fully participate in capitalist dynamics while retaining the appearance of mental sanity. . . It enables you to fully participate in the frantic pace of the capitalist game while sustaining the perception that you are not really in it; that you are well aware of how worthless this spectacle is; and that what really matters to you is the peace of the inner Self to which you know you can always withdraw.[10]

In this way liberal and conservative middle-class ideologies can comfortably merge within the material structure of capitalism while simultaneously (and perhaps superficially) proclaiming or posturing an antagonistic relationship. Bateman encompasses these sides of social life in capitalism as a health guru who feels and looks great because he "believes in taking care of himself" while manifesting his appearance of success through commodities and enacting violence via methods of subjective detachment.

It fits Bateman's character to praise the music of Whitney Houston, particularly his favorite Whitney song "The Greatest Love of All." He describes it as such:

> But Whitney's talent is restored with the overwhelming "The Greatest Love of All," one of the best, most powerful songs ever written about self-preservation and dignity. From the first line to the last, it's a state-of-the-art ballad about believing in yourself. It's a powerful statement . . . Its universal message crosses all boundaries and instills one with the hope that it's not too late for us to better ourselves, to act kinder. Since it's impossible in the world we live in to empathize with others, we can always empathize with ourselves. It's an important message, crucial really, and it's beautifully stated on this album.[11]

Bateman's assessment of the song perfectly expresses the superficial capitalist ideology of believing in one's self and the inability to empathize with others. We are all unique and each of us sees and feels things just a little bit (or maybe a lot) different from everybody else in the world. No one can truly empathize with other individuals. The internal contradiction of aiming to better ourselves with being kinder illuminates the paradoxical relationship of self-care/self-love and other-care/other-love. An emphasis and practice of self-care/self-love cannot produce love and care for others. The contradictions reveal themselves within Bateman's own description. It is impossible to be empathetic, but somehow we can be kinder. The term self-preservation alludes to the often misinterpreted survival of the species via Social Darwinism but also communicates something deeper about the nature of life within the capitalist mode of production that creates a system where individuals must literally engage in self-preservation. The society does not and cannot produce dignified people, so you must do it yourself.

The song lyrics display a striking similarity of the rhetoric that came from the ascending neoliberal capitalism of the early 1980s. The song begins with the seemingly innocent words of inspiration about children. "I believe the children are the future. Teach them well and let them lead the way. Show them all the beauty they possess inside." But the hollow and stereotypical pop culture niceties of the song suddenly develop into an egocentric diatribe of egoistic self-love against community and collectivity. It continues:

> Everybody searching for a hero
> People need someone to look up to
> I never found anyone who fulfill my needs
> A lonely place to be
> And so I learned to depend on me[12]

In total capitalist egotism, she can only depend on herself. Students have internalized this ethical value. It continues:

> I decided long ago
> Never to walk in anyone's shadows
> If I fail, if I succeed
> At least I'll live as I believe
> Because the greatest
> Love of all is happening to me
> I found the greatest
> Love of all inside of me
> Learning to love yourself
> It is the greatest love of all[13]

It is easy to see why this is Patrick Bateman's favorite song. It smoothly glides along the cutthroat conservative notions of individual responsibility (success and failure) to the liberal self-care/self-love (learn to love yourself). It represents a total detachment from the social and the collective and focuses on the internal subjective reality of loving the self, a love that is objectively greater than the love of others and the love exchanged between people! This song epitomizes the ideological values that emerge from capitalist material conditions. In fact, learning to love yourself is the only option and does not have to be learned in the traditional sense. It simply occurs. While learning to love others . . .

When students aim for confidence from the subjectivity of the personal mindset and through consumer means, they become disengaged from the social where looking and feeling good, through an emphasis on the self, allows for the continuation of violence via the capitalist mode of production. This can be described as narcissism, hedonistic nihilism, and/or ethical solipsism, but regardless, it emerges from the material conditions of capitalism. *American Psycho* demonstrates how these ways of being materialize and dominate every avenue of social and cultural practice. By default, those of the middle class are all Patrick Bateman individuals and their entire culture is psychotic. Then, they impose it onto the working class.

The two examples above explain how individualism operates as both the natural outgrowth of the material conditions of capitalism and as an ideological basis for student perspectives and teacher pedagogy. The first involves the responsibilization of each individual as maker and chooser of one's own destiny of success or failure. The second involves a subjective internal experience of pseudo-transcendence (transcendence of class antagonisms and subsequent violence).

In the first example, Downs' seeks guidance from the logic of reality television. Tim Gunn serves as the giver of knowledge or a fashion designer crossed with Dr. Phil. This is what people get in capitalism. Entertainment, consumerism, and psychology, all cut throat and loaded with hyper-doses of tough love, wrapped into one package.

Educators must displace the role of the individual in the classroom and develop a collective structure. Each student must deeply engage with every other student to the point where the success of one is the success of all and the failure of one is the failure of all. This can be done in a very practical way, such as collective grading through collective projects and the elimination of individual tests, quizzes, and assignments, altogether. Like the planning, executing, and completion of giant public works projects, each course could be structured as a giant collective public works project that requires collective activity and mass cooperation.

The obvious problem with a classroom/school structured collectively involves the individualism and cut throat structure students will face outside of the educational institution. Therefore, educators must aim to change the structure outside of the institution. Changing the classroom without changing the system outside of the classroom will be fruitless, and this applies directly to fighting against the cult of individualism of the dominant economic and subsequent cultural system.

Capitalism & Class

In capitalism, success is measured in dollars and commodities. As educators we must be honest about this reality and avoid sentimentalizing and moralizing success within capitalism. Morality emerges from the capitalist mode of production, which means competition foregrounds our morality. This fact undermines notions of success that revolve around love of family, commitment to friends, minor personal achievements, and insignificant community involvement. When we sentimentalize or moralize these things, they point to a lack within capitalism. Since selling our labor power determines our ways of being, we must rationalize our objective powerlessness by emphasizing the intangible forms of success we build.

To be more specific, when asked how to define success students will claim that success to them does not specifically relate to financial success, but rather to the successes of family life and so forth. Some students' note:

> To me success means taking care of family the best I can by working hard and making sure they always have a place to live and food to eat. To me this is the definition of success.
>
> Success is how hard you try and not what you have. I am successful because I have love from my family and friends. Even though we don't have a lot, we make the best of what we do have. The most successful thing in the world is loyalty to friends and family.
>
> I don't care about being rich or having an expensive car or a big house. I think people who have that stuff have a tougher life then me. I am successful because I work hard for what I have and I take care of my six month old daughter. Success should not be measured by cars or houses, but by being a good person and working hard.

Countless students' repeat these sorts of emotional and sentimental assertions about success. Again, this is because they, especially those of the working class, objectively lack the most significant type of success in capitalism, which is financial success. In reality, those of the working class have no other choice but to redefine success sentimentally and morally. Instead of changing the structure of the system to where notions of success emerge that revolve around the value of collectivity, cooperation, and security, we tend to moralize what the system inherently lacks. Again, educators and students fall victim to this sentimentalizing and moralizing. In fact, it is difficult to do anything else.

As educators, we must focus on changing the economic structure and avoid encouraging students to aim to succeed within the limits of capitalism. This is particularly important with students of the working class. Inform students directly:

> In terms of economics, there are a couple simple things that make for the drastic class distinction we see in the country and world. One is private property ownership, which allows for some to own the most valuable resources and so forth, which means that everybody else has to work for those people because they are objectively unable to subsist since they don't own anything. This leads to the second thing, which is wage labor. Us working-class folks, since we don't own anything, have only our labor power to sell as a commodity on the market to those who do own everything. Therefore, our horizon is limited to our labor. Third, there is the profit motive, which means that those who do own everything have to keep generating profits at all cost. If one business or company doesn't maximize profits, then another one will take over. Finally, competition is at the foundation of it all, which means we all compete against each other rather than cooperate. Workers compete for jobs, promotions and so forth and businesses compete for domination.

> So, it is structural, not moral. The structure of the economic system results in economic class distinction and antagonism. It is structural so it has nothing to do with effort and attitude or hard work.

In terms of honesty about capitalism, educators must avoid cheerleading toward inclusion into a higher level of capitalist success while also avoiding the sentimental and moral rationalizing. Simply state the objective structural reality of the capitalist system. It is also unnecessary to emotionalize the plight of folks from the working class. Yes, the predicament is authentically sad, but again, we are not talking about morality; we are talking about structure. Of course it is sad that people in Nigeria are so desperate that at a great risk to their health and life they siphon oil off of established pipelines where they end up covered in oil and breathe in the most toxic of fumes daily.[14] We can always refer to Friedrich Engels *Condition of the Working Class in England*, or Marx's long and detailed descriptions the working conditions of the working day in *Capital Volume 1* or even a Michael Moore film like *Sicko*, but the problem with moralizing the issue with emotionally charged content is that it involves a detachment from structure. Many students do not see themselves as exploited, particularly as exploited as the Nigerians or the Victorian workers. Therefore, students view this material as "those unfortunate people out there somewhere or back then sometime." This could have the opposite affect or an unintended appreciation for their relatively higher standard of living in capitalism.

Noble-izing poverty, the working class, and the working poor presents another problem in the approach of liberal educators of the middle class to understand and articulate class structure and exploitation (conservatives simply blame the poor for their own plight). This type of sentimentality and morality exists on par with the old notion of the "noble savage" and depoliticizes and even eliminates questions of class. This sort of moralizing appears more detrimental than "rags to riches" tropes (or rages to middle-class tropes, e.g. if *you* work hard enough, etc.).

Basically, poverty demoralizes. Back in 1866, the *Children's Employment Commission: Fifth Report* notes:

> The greatest evil of the system that employs young girls on this sort of work, consists in this, that, as a rule, it chains them fast from childhood for the whole of their afterlife to the most abandoned rabble. They become rough, foul mouthed boys, before Nature has taught them that they are women. Clothed in a few dirty rags, the legs naked far above the knees, hair and face besmeared with dirt, they learn to treat all feelings of decency and of shame with contempt. During meal times they lie at full length in the fields, or watch the boys bathing in a neighboring canal. Their heavy day's work at length completed, they put on better clothes, and accompany the men to the public houses. That excessive insobriety is prevalent from childhood upwards among the whole of this class, is only natural. The worst is that the brick makers despair of themselves. You might as well, said one of

> the better kind to a chaplain of Southallfield, try to raise and improve the devil as a brick maker.[15]

This passage from Marx's *Capital Volume 1* is not intended to make any specific claims about sexual morality or appropriate gendered behavior. Rather, it illustrates, from the Victorian perspective the acknowledgement that the manufacture and factory systems that pushed the working class into concretely unhealthy and dangerous conditions, resulted in a demoralized working-class population. Conversely, if these working-class girls were born and raised in the context of the middle class, the likelihood of them becoming demoralized (regardless of one's relative concepts of morality) appears small.

The commission's report comes from a Christian sense of morality but nonetheless highlights the fact that material context related to economic class largely determines the behavior and activity of people. The capitalist system chains them fast from childhood for the whole of their afterlife (life after child labor) to the most abandoned rabble (indelible marker of class). Those raised in the circumstances of the middle class find this concept hard to understand. The higher one is on the economic pyramid, the more profound the misunderstanding. For instance, it is difficult for those higher on the economic pyramid to conceptualize looting during urban protests and uprisings. They ask, "Why would they destroy their own neighborhoods?" or "Why would they steal from their own businesses?" The answer lies in demoralization, which stems from economic powerlessness connected to class structure. It also lies in the fact that consumer items represent identity status or sign value. The capitalist system promotes the ownership of consumer objects and thus protest means taking consumer objects, the most valued things in the society and culture. In other words, the essence of capitalism permeates the protests.

In terms of black market capitalism, which emerges from class structure, the need for money for survival, and the constant propagation of money as status (or being someone and not no one), it is easy to see the mirroring of "legitimate" or "legal" capitalist behavior. Essentially, cutthroat capitalist activity, such as by the oil, pharmaceutical, arms, and agricultural industries, provide a model for black markets like drugs, guns, human smuggling and so forth, not to mention that "legitimate" and "legal" industries benefit from the black market. The main point is that the demoralized human via class structure lives within a hybrid universe of abject poverty amidst abject wealth. The poverty demoralizes in one way and the wealth demoralizes in another. They merge and create the entirely demoralized populations. We can rationalize all of it and, subsequently, we can noble-ize it when it is good (the impoverished people who work hard, etc.) but also condemn it when it is bad (the impoverished people who engage in black market capitalism or "crime"). Like the "noble savage," the impoverished, working poor, or working class, do not win in any of these equations. The systemic structure or the material conditions which create the demoralization never gets attacked.

Educators must attack the system that creates poverty. Noble-izing some of the working class and rationalizing some of the working class offers no solutions to the underlying problems. Žižek provides a succinct description, "I don't like this [liberal] romantic false idea that suffering purifies you, that it makes you a noble person. It does not! . . . [On the contrary] it makes you do anything to survive."[16] When that "anything" is legal, the tendency is to noble-ize; when that "anything" is "illegal," the tendency is to rationalize. Neither tendency works.

For example, when a highly paid professional athlete from the working class commits a crime the middle class might ask, "Why would someone who makes that much money do something so stupid?" Again, this constitutes a clear misunderstanding of how class structure works or a lack in understanding of how class becomes indelibly ingrained into people. Winning the lottery does not eliminate the formative years of life already lived. Mark Fisher refers to the indelible marker of class in his article, "Good for Nothing." He refers to David Smail:

> Smail describes how the marks of class are designed to be indelible. For those who from birth are taught to think of themselves as lesser, the acquisition of qualifications or wealth will seldom be sufficient to

> erase, either in their own minds or in the minds of others, the primordial sense of worthlessness that marks them so early in life. Someone who moves out of the social sphere they are 'supposed' to occupy is always in danger of being overcome by feelings of vertigo, panic and horror.[17]

The fact is that under the current capitalist economic structure almost all folks of the working class will never metaphorically win the lottery and become rich (and will probably never achieve basic economic security). The fact is that under the current capitalist economic structure most folks of the working class will remain working class and working poor their entire lives. The best folks of the working class can do is to move up a rung on the ladder or a level on the pyramid. For educators, it is best to acknowledge these facts and aim to change the current economic structure rather than to expend energy into moving the working class up a rung or level. The fact that most formal educators come from the middle class does not help.

As with all the aspects present here, the middle class do not constitute individuals to be analyzed and understood on an individual basis. Instead, the middle class constitute a vague catch-all group that describes what the working class simply do not constitute. To quantify class by salary or assets creates too many difficulties, although class is not entirely qualitative. For instance, public school teachers might represent the working class in a very concrete way. They must work. They have only their labor to sell. They do not own any means of production. Yet, public school teachers may be of the middle class because they, more than likely, come from the middle class. The (purposeful) muddling of class, e.g. everybody is middle class, complicates the distinctions. Therefore, it proves most productive to put aside these complications and perhaps measure class by background and level of security.

Competition

One the most destructive aspects of the capitalist mode of production is competition. Subsequently, it is also one of the shadiest embedded ideological beliefs educators and students hold. The idea of competition is understood as a natural way of being. Of course, this may be a continuation of the Social Darwinism that emerged as an idea from the capitalist mode of production during the mid-nineteenth century. The idea that competition is the natural order of things is deeply implanted into the minds of students of both the working and middle class. It pervades the entire capitalist society, in which students and educators find themselves. We concretely compete for everything. Therefore, the material conditions and the capitalist mode of production form the ideological beliefs about competition.

As with other deeply embedded ways of being within capitalism, competition carries a powerful message about progress, success, and reality. In other words, competition brings progress, success, and shapes perceptions about reality. The reality is that life is a series of endless competitions, but without it human beings would not progress or reach the heights of success, whether individually or societally. Students, without any hesitation, will cite the success of Bill Gates or Steve Jobs as evidence of the benefits of competition, the forward movement of progress, and the benefits for society. Advanced technology illustrates how far humans have come and without individuals who strove and struggled to make their dreams a reality, humans would live less desirable lives.

Obviously, this is a common narrative that comes from advertising in the tech world (and other industries), but it is also a common notion about the nature of human beings. Since competition appears to be the natural order of things, there must be a corresponding lack in the material conditions of society. This lack is cooperation. Students and educators carry the assumption that life must be a struggle and that from this struggle individuals who work hard enough will overcome the obstacles presented during the struggle and, therefore, succeed. So struggle is presupposed. Obstacles are presupposed. Individual hard work is presupposed. Proposing to students that life does not have to be an individual struggle, nor filled with obstacles or hard work surprises students.

To highlight how competition foregrounds students thoughts about the world, consider this list of quotes from students when asked to provide a meaningful quote to share with their classmates:

> "The mindset isn't about seeking a result, it's more about the process of getting to that result. It's about the journey and the approach. It's a way of life. I do think that it's important, in all endeavors, to have that mentality." Kobe Bryant
>
> "You make mistakes. Mistakes don't make you." Maxwell Maltz
>
> "Suffer the pain of discipline or suffer the pain of regret."
>
> "Your attitude determines your direction."
>
> "I've failed over and over and over again in my life. And that is why I succeed." Michael Jordan
>
> "Everything happens for a reason."
>
> "Yesterday is history, tomorrow is a mystery, but today is a gift. That is why it is called present." Kung Fu Panda
>
> "Everything comes to you at the right time. Be patient and trust in the process."
>
> "Do not be embarrassed by your failures, learn from them and start again."
>
> "Remember, tomorrow is promised to no one." Walter Payton

> "Success is not final, failure is not fatal: it is the courage to continue that counts." Winston Churchill

> "Lo que no me mata me alimenta," which translates to "What doesn't kill me feeds me" Frida Kahlo

> "Let me tell you something you already know: the world ain't all sunshine and rainbows. It's a very mean and nasty place and I don't care how tough you are, it will beat you to your knees and keep you there permanently. If you let it, you, me, or nobody is gonna hit as hard as life but it ain't about hard you can hit, it's about how hard you can get hit and keep going." Sylvester Stallone

> "Your work is going to fill a large part of your life, and the only way to be truly satisfied is to do what you believe is great work. And the only way to do great work is to love what you do. If you haven't found it yet, keep looking. Don't settle. As with all matters of the heart, you'll know when you find it. So keep looking until you find it. Don't settle." Steve Jobs

Students always highlight the struggle, the obstacles, and the grandiose individual effort required to overcome them. Students rarely present quotes about collective efforts or cooperative endeavors. Notice also that there exists a hands-off notion of fate, as if the universe decides one's fate, or that as long as the individual does their part of working hard that their destiny will prove successful. Of course, if it doesn't then that same logic of fate also supplies the answer. Either I did not work hard enough or my fate decided failure (a coherent tautology).

The above quotes come from students objectively of the working class. For the middle class, this entire tautology supports their notions of success. Moreover, it seems obvious that the success of individuals of the middle class is *because they are individuals of the middle class.* Regardless, they believe that their success comes from their hard work and their ability to rise above the rest and not because of their material circumstances from birth. In essence, folks of the working class *must compete*, but for people from the middle class, competition serves as an illusion of competition, which reinforces their own objective class advantages.

Regardless, educators must emphasize the objective failure of competition as a basis for economic organization. Anyone who has read chapter 13 of Marx's *Capital Volume 1*, knows that cooperation also permeates the capitalist mode of production, but as long as the capitalist mode of production dictates economic organization, this cooperation simply serves capital. The material structure involves untold forms of highly technical and finely tuned cooperation, yet notions of competition dominates. Why? Because we compete while we cooperate, or we cooperate while we compete. The cooperation proves secondary because the competition means concrete personal survival (keeping the job) while the cooperation means productivity (efficiency, etc.). All the negative aspects of competition fall upon the worker while all the positive aspects of cooperation flow to the capitalist.

Communication

Finally, mass communication offers a clear target to pinpoint in order to combat capitalism. Rather than praising the utility, efficiency, or even the organizing possibilities of mass communication, educators must relay the notion of radical non-communication. Like the dialectic of cooperation and competition that emerges from the capitalist mode of production, the same sort of dialectic emerges from mass communication in the form of the social and the antisocial. Only changing the mode of communication can result in a dramatic shift from the antisocial to the social.

People communicate constantly through social media, text messages, and so on, yet society becomes antisocial and combative. Information becomes both true and false in real time while historical time and its vital context disappears. As Baudrillard notes when discussing the Holocaust:

> In historical time, the [Holocaust] took place and the evidence is there. But we are no longer in historical time; we are now in real time, and in real time there is no longer any evidence of anything whatever. The holocaust will never be verified in real time. Holocaust denial is, therefore, absurd in its own logic, but by its very absurdity it sheds light on the irruption of another dimension, paradoxically termed 'real time,' a dimension in which, paradoxically, objective reality disappears. And not just the reality of the present event, but also that of past and future events. Everything now runs out its course in a state of

> simultaneity, so that acts no longer find their meaning, effects no longer find their cause, and history can no longer be an object of reflection.[18]

With the advent of hyper-mass communication comes the loss of historical time and without historical time comes the loss of the material basis of history. In fact, materialism loses its grip as a means to apprehend objective reality, since it disappears with people inside a cell of mass communication. Reinserting history into the overall landscape of human economy requires an objective stance against communication. Grand projects of economic change can never emerge from the social relations inherent in social media and other technological forms of instantaneous and constant communication.

Furthermore, since the economic base foregrounds mass communication in every possible way (e.g. social media as productive labor that produces profits) an anti-social media means a rejection of productive labor and the greater potential for the social to reemerge. Again, by analogy, the means of production also includes the vectors of mass communication in their most concrete form and just like productive activity that benefits the few capitalists from human labor power, communication must be (re)appropriated to collective productive activity that benefits all workers. It cannot simply be assumed that mass communication is either benign or offers possibilities for radical change, but radical change itself must include the change in the material structure of mass communication (how, how much, and for what we communicate). In other words, all use of mass communication media directly correlates to perpetuating and consolidating capitalist power. Therefore, the underlying structure of mass communication must be changed so that humans can engage in mass communication without directly empowering capitalism.

Education must address the core of capitalist power that includes the concrete material reality and its subsequent ideology about policing, private property, individualism, competition, and mass communication. All of these aspects of capitalism disrupt and foreclose the potential of a new and better material economic base for society. Only through radical changes in the material economic base and the capitalist mode of production and its social relations can education become revolutionary and liberatory. Therefore, all of these goals must be actively pursued simultaneously both in and out of the classroom and/or on and off the campus. As long as policing is justified and detached from private property or as long as private property is presupposed; and as long as individualism is privileged and competition is assumed; and as long as constant mass communication occurs as productive activity; and without a dramatic seizure of the means of production, education remains an isolated endeavor that supports the classism and the other objective dangers of capitalism.

---

[1] https://www.govinfo.gov/content/pkg/FR-2020-01-17/pdf/2020-00858.pdf

[2] Zack Friedman, "78% Of Workers Live Paycheck To Paycheck," https://www.forbes.com/sites/zackfriedman/2019/01/11/live-paycheck-to-paycheck-government-shutdown/

[3] https://www.statista.com/statistics/585152/people-shot-to-death-by-us-police-by-race/

[4]https://watson.brown.edu/costsofwar/files/cow/imce/papers/2021/Suitt_Suicides_Costs%20of%20War_June%2021%202021.pdf

[5] The term "unconsciously" is used to denote that the attitudes, decisions, practices, and ideas of educators are foregrounded or determined by the material conditions of the capitalist society.

[6] Maggie Downs. "Tim Gunn and a Leaky Shower: Welcome to My Life, Little Guy," *The Washington Post*, July 1, 2015.

[7] The one difference that may be noted when we compare Patrick Bateman with the YouTubers is that the YouTubers are not violent. This is because in capitalism the violence is done by other entities within the material structure, such as domestic and international policing, mass incarceration, and so on. Bateman represents the entire spectrum of capitalism while the YouTubers represent a part of capitalism.

[8] Fisher, *Capitalist Realism*, 73.

[9] https://zizek.uk/the-buddhist-ethic-and-the-spirit-of-global-capitalism/, Slavoj Žižek, "The Buddhist Ethic and the Spirit of Global Capitalism," August 10, 2012.

[10] http://cabinetmagazine.org/issues/2/zizek.php, Slavoj Žižek, "From Western Marxism To Western Buddhism," Spring 2001.

[11] Bret Easton Ellis, *American Psycho*, 252-256.

[12] Whitney Houston, Lyrics to "The Greatest Love of All," https://genius.com/Whitney-houston-greatest-love-of-all-lyrics

[13] Ibid.

[14] "Deadliest Roads: Nigeria," https://www.youtube.com/watch?v=_OfHGtSkZG8

[15] Qtd. in Karl Marx, *Capital Volume* 1, 593-94.

[16] https://qz.com/767751/marxist-philosopher-slavoj-zizek-on-europes-refugee-crisis-the-left-is-wrong-to-pity-and-romanticize-migrants/, Annalisa Merelli, "Marxist Philosopher Slavoj Žižek Explains Why we shouldn't Pity or Romanticize Refugees," September 9, 2016.

[17] https://theoccupiedtimes.org/?p=12841, Mark Fisher, "Good for Nothing," March 19, 2014.

[18] Jean Baudrillard, *Screened Out*, 108.

www.ingramcontent.com/pod-product-compliance
Lightning Source LLC
LaVergne TN
LVHW050616100826
845148LV00011B/1610

* 9 7 8 0 5 7 8 9 6 8 7 6 6 *